Filey

A History of The Town and its People.

W.M. Rhodes

Filey A History of The Town and its People.

W.M. Rhodes ©2017.

ISBN 978-09957752-0-6

ISBN 978-09957752-8-2

First Edition 19th May 2017

Second Edition July 2018.

Dedication

This book is dedicated to the people who have lost their lives at sea, and for the brave volunteers who risk their own lives attempting to rescue them.

What though the sea be calm

Trust to the shore; Ships have been drown'd

Where late they danced before.

(Robert Herrick)

Contents

Acknowledgements

This is the second edition of *Filey A History of the Town and Its People*. There were a couple more stories and photographs that I wanted to add to this version.

I would like to express my appreciation to Stephen Eblet, Joanne Cammish, Marilyn Briggs, Ian Nisbet, Filey Town Council and all the people who gave their permission to allow me to reproduce photographs for this book. Some of the photographs are old and out of copyright. Thank you to Edward Waterson for inspiring me to research and write the story of North Cliff Villa and Miss Elinor Clarke.

Thank you to my team especially my editor Maureen Vincent-Northam, and Jeannie Williams for proofreading.

To my husband, Paul, and our children Kristian, Becky & Zoe, their partners and all our grandchildren.

To all the people of Filey-past and present who have made Filey-The Jewel of The Yorkshire Coast.

W M Rhodes.

Filey 2018.

Filey's Roman Presence

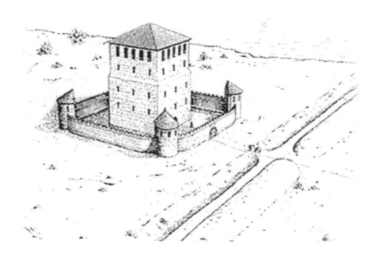

Arguably, one of the most significant events that happened in Britain is the Roman invasion. For over 400 years (and still evident today) the Romans have influenced our language, culture, architecture and geography. Prior to the Roman occupation, Britain had a diminished sense of identity, people tended to be insular and stayed close to their local tribes. After the Romans came to town inhabitants were aware that their national mythology was defined, and every person in the land was mindful of their 'Britishness'. In addition, the Welsh were conscious that they were Britain's natural heirs. Whereas the Scots and the Irish were equally proud that they had not been conquered and occupied by the Romans.

To administer their people, the Romans built towns and connected these towns together by building roads. These roads were constructed on foundations of clay, chalk and gravel, flat stones were then laid on top. These roads tended to slope in the middle to man-made ditches at either side to allow rainwater to drain. Roads were built as straight as possible to enable Roman soldiers to travel as quickly as possible, ensuring that there were no enemies hiding in any winding unseen areas. The roads were so well built that many of them can still be seen today.

In Yorkshire, the main Roman town was Eboracum (York as we know it today). Malton was a Roman garrison named Derventio, which was a town of great importance and a base for troops who could easily be deployed if required. To protect themselves from land invasion, the Romans built walls around their cities, preventing fierce barbarian attacks from tribes such as The Huns from Mongolia and Germanic Tribes from the Danube River. To protect their towns from an invasion by sea, early warning look-out stations were built along the coast. These stations could signal each other and alert any sign of danger.

For many years, renowned archaeologists have written articles and journals to try to prove that Filey Bay was the Portus Felix or Sinus Salutaris of the Romans and that Flamborough Head the Ocellum Promontorium. However, these are theories that continue to be debated. Further speculation remains that Filey was the territorial home to one of the Celtic Parisi tribes (there were four in the North). The Parisi was a small group of people who farmed the chalk hills of Yorkshire and who also traded by boat, most probably a longboat. As a tribe, the Parisi was not as powerful as their neighbours the Brigantes but were ahead in culture and taught their unrefined neighbours about style, and culinary matters. The Parisi were known to live in British style houses with ornaments and pottery.

The Parisi tribe were originally from Gaul and shared their name with the people who lived in France around the area we know today as Paris.

Despite being responsible for the name of the French capital, it is not clear if they shared any other links with the French. This tribe were distinctive, as unlike many others living in Britain between 300 and100 B.C., the Parisi buried their dead under small barrows that were surrounded by small ditches. Some nobles were buried with their chariots, which is the 'Arras' culture and a similar style to that of the French and Germans. Another burial style involved a dead person being placed in a grave and a fine sword placed alongside him, while three spears were then thrust into his chest. These unusual burial rituals ceased around 43-45AD. It appears that the Parisi was an ununiformed tribe, who along with their neighbours the Brigantes did not defend themselves against the arrival of the Romans.

Reports show that Filey was once occupied by the Romans during their invasion of England, as in October 1857, following weeks of severe rain a landslip occurred on Carr Naze; three hundred yards from 'The Summer House' (once an attraction of the 'Spaw Well' on Carr Naze in the mid-nineteenth century) and close to the second flight of steps beyond Agony Point, when a painter named Mr Jeffrey Wilson discovered the remains of a Roman Fort. Here, he uncovered large stones, which were generally in a rough state with tooled surfaces set on a foundation of puddled clay. This walled area was rectangular and about 60 feet long by 25 feet wide, with one door opening to the land.

Within these walls were five shaft base stones, one with a carving of a running deer and on a second a calf who was about to lie down. Also, found, were the remains of burnt wood, a spearhead, with burnt bones, which lay on the floor, together with a piece of shale or shaly slate inscribed, CAESAR SE…and QVAM SPE. Coins were also found, which were brass and had become greatly corroded. It is reported that these coins bore the mark of Constantine and Constans.

The beacons were arranged at the corners of a square measuring about 17 feet with one stone in the centre. It is generally accepted that these stones would have formed the bases for pillars on which rested a superstructure. Most probably, there was a raised platform which supported a lighted beacon. Conceivably, the beacon's attendant and his family lived nearby to light the beacon when required and keep it bright and strong to carry a signal north and south to warn the ancient mariner of the dangerous rocks, and to welcome back the midnight wanderer.

On discovery, it appeared that the Roman structure had been severely damaged, and then set on fire, suggesting that it had been overwhelmed by raiders, presumably from the sea. These five stones are on display in The Crescent Gardens and are all clear indications that a Roman township existed in the area.

The following year, Rev. Richard Burke, the then owner of Carr Naze, allowed local antiquarian Dr William Smithson Cortis to excavate his land. To the south-eastward of the Spa Well, Cortis unearthed a variety of pottery which was typical of the Roman era, one with a green glaze, and a larger wine-vase formed from red clay ornamented with painted scrolls. One piece of Samian was unearthed, together with buckles, pins, a part of a sword, a sharpening stone, beads etc. Unfortunately, what has happened to these artefacts is not known.

In 1893, Mr Robert M Robson writes in the Journal of the Society of Architects, of the discovery of nine oak posts found on Filey Brigg by Messrs R & W Cappleman. This discovery suggested that the posts were the remains of a landing stage used by the Romans when Filey was one of their mooring stations. He also implies that there is other evidence pointing to this such as the Roman Roads, Spittal Rocks, Fess Rocks, Quay Rocks, and the artificially flattened surface of the Binks on the north side of the bay. However, despite these findings, to date, there is no definite confirmation that Roman occupation existed in Filey.

Roman stones now situated in Crescent Gardens

Domesday and Early Settlement

The earliest documented evidence of Filey comes from The Domesday Book, which was compiled in 1068 CE on the instructions of William the Conqueror primarily for tax purposes. This review was known as the 'great survey of England' and determined how much land and livestock each of the counties' landowners owned, how much it was worth, and how much tax they should pay. These records show that at the end of the Viking period, Filey is recorded for the first time as a very small village occupied by less than fifty people. It states that Filey was worth a reasonable income, with access to good quality timber which was ideal for construction.

The Norman Conquest found Filey belonging to the rebellious Earl Tosti. The Domesday survey describes Filey as forfeited to the King and was by him given to one of his faithful followers and relatives Walter de Gant, who was born in 1080 in Bridlington.

It is impossible to know just how old Filey is, it may have been founded between 878 and 1080 or possibly earlier. It is known that the Danes settled in the North between 878-1080. Therefore, it could be that Filey was founded by this North Germanic tribe who originally came to England as Vikings. However, at this time Filey was basically one large farm, and the name Filey itself suggests that it had more of an Anglican influence rather than a Danish one, as generally farms founded by Danes usually ended with the suffix 'by' such as Whitby or Selby. So, this could mean that the Danes did not have the influence in Filey as first thought. However, this is not conclusive. Interestingly, we can detect a strong Scandinavian influence in the dialect of many Filey people, for instance, in terms such as 'garth' meaning garden, '-uh-wand' as an expression of surprise or 'where-be-orzit' meaning who or where do you come from? It could be that the Danish Vikings figure more in the ancestry of Filey than we first thought. Furthermore, we can certainly see the Norse influence in the fishing cobles used by the Filey fishermen who adopted the Danish skill of boatbuilding by using the 'clinker' method of building which involved the overlapping of planks of wood to construct sea-worthy boats.

It is proposed that during the Middle Ages, and somewhere near the site of today's church, there once stood an ancient Saxon church dedicated to St Bartholomew. This was most likely in the field behind the present church. However, by the 16th century, this church was in ruins. To date, there is no further physical evidence to suggest anything happening in Filey until the building of St. Oswald's Church around 1150 CE. So, there is a gap in our knowledge of any recorded activity in Filey for a good five centuries – roughly between 500 and 1000 CE.

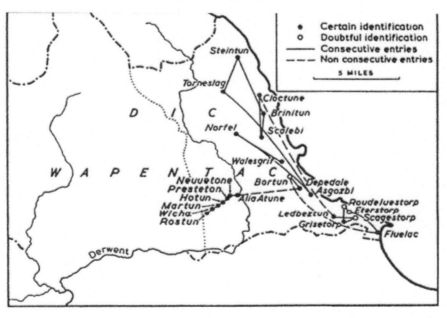

North Filey - The Buck and The Beckwith Families

As discussed we have no knowledge of what was happening in Filey between 500 and 1000 CE. However, we do know that St Oswald's church was built around 1150, but there is only a sparse understanding of the community of Filey around this time. For Filey to be mentioned in the Domesday book, we can assume that there must have been a community there in the time following the Norman Conquest. However, the Domesday Book does not mention either a monastery or a church in Filey. Therefore, we can assume that the church was built to serve an existing community. Whereas, nowadays, the church is virtually isolated on the north of Church Ravine dividing it from the rest of the town and the community. It does not seem feasible that a church of this magnitude would have been built on the 'wrong' side of the tracks, where no population resided. Afterall, Filey inhabitants would have had to clamber up and down steep cliffs just to go to church, which doesn't seem feasible.

According to Cole, (182167) there are old records (which he does not specify) which speak of the north and south of Filey as two separate entities, and that there are many foundations of old buildings near St Oswald's church. [1] However, no documentation exists to confirm this.

---

1 Cole. J. The Antiquities of Filey. 1827.

Over the years, excavations have taken place to ascertain if indeed a church or a manor house existed on land to the north of Filey. In 1927, an archaeological dig was undertaken by surveyors Clay, Robson and Smith, who indicated that there was a possibility of a manor house in this area, belonging to the Buck family. It has been suggested, that this manor house could have been in the same area where Church Cliff Farm is now. Also, that there was an original smaller church, together with the possibility that St Oswald's is built directly on top of the original Filey church. Further excavations took place in Queen Street in the 1970s, where it is claimed that medieval remains were found. However, there is still a significant gap between approx. 300 years from the building of St Oswald's Church and the community of Queen Street, (King Street, Town Street) Filey's oldest recorded street.

Land immediately in front of Church Cliff Farm, could this be the place of Filey's original settlement?

Excavations at Church Cliff Farm.

The Bucks & The Beckwith's

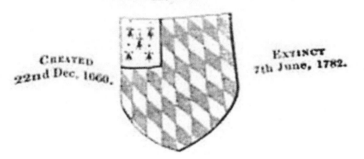

BUCK, OF HAMBY-GRANGE.

CREATED
22nd Dec. 1660.

EXTINCT
7th June, 1782.

It is said that a manor house existed in 'north Filey' that could have belonged to the Buck family. Later records show, that Sir John Buck of Hamby-Grange was knighted by King Charles 1st with several others at Whitehall on 23rd July 1603 before his majesty's coronation. John Buck married Elizabeth Green, the daughter and heir of William Green Esq of Filey. The couple lived at Hamby Grange, Leverton, Lincolnshire. John Buck held the office of Sheriff of Lincolnshire from 1619-1620 and later became Sheriff of York. The couple had a son also named John Buck who married three times. He was created 1st Baronet Buck, of Hamby Grange, co. Lincoln [England] on 22 December 1660. He also held the office of Sheriff of Lincolnshire from 1663 to 1664.

The Beckwith's derived their name from Lady Dame Beckwith Bruce, daughter of Sir William Bruce, the third Lord of Annandale, whose Lordship and lands he had inherited from his ancestor. Dame was also the half-sister of Sir Robert the Bruce of Skelton Castle, the progenitor of the Royal Bruce's of Scotland. Her father, William de Bruce possessed large estates in the north of England. Lady Beckwith Bruce possessed by inheritance an estate or Manor of land called Beckwith in the old Anglo-Saxon Beckworth from "Beck" a brook and "Worth" an estate. In 1226, Dame married Sir Hercules de Malebisse and requested that upon her marriage, her husband changed his name by deed to Beckwith. Sir Hercules was the great-grandson of Sir Hugo de Malebisse c. 1066 who held lands in the time of William the Conqueror.

Adam Beckwith, Lord of Clint (b.1405) married Elizabeth de Malebisse (b. 1406) and thus united the two branches of the De Malebisse families after a separation of over three hundred years. Adam was the son of Thomas Beckwith. The couple's eldest son Sir William married the daughter of Sir John Baskerville, who, in turn, was succeeded by his son Thomas Beckwith of Clint, Thomas married the daughter and co-heiress of W.M Haslerton, and thus became Lord of the Manor of Filey, Muston and Thorp, which his wife had inherited from Havisia, the daughter and co-heiress of Ralph de Neville.

Another branch of the Beckwith family was Mathew Beckwith of Tanfield, who was a captain in the Parliamentary Army. Mathew married Elizabeth Buck of Filey, the daughter of John Buck. The couple did not live in Filey, but in Tanfield, where Mathew died in 1679. It is interesting to see just how these families are connected, and the influence they had in the small town of Filey.

Filey: Possible Origins of its Name

The origins of the name 'Filey' are not precisely known. It could be that it originated from the word Fucelac meaning 'the bay where the birds are'. However, this is disputed, and reports suggest that this spelling is misread. Thus, according to Sir Henry Ellis's edition of the Domesday Book, the name Fiuelac is the correct spelling, as it refers to 'five pools' which includes 'The Emperors Bath' in which Constantine the Great is believed to have bathed in over one thousand and seven hundred years ago, (a claim that has never been substantiated). Interestingly, the suffix 'lac' is an ancient Northumbrian word for wood, which confirms the findings written in this famous book. Also, there was a great forest in 'Scalby' in support of this.

Further claims to the origin of the name have been made over the years. In the thirteenth century, the name was written as 'Fyvele' then 'Fyveley'. Some people suggested that the name was Fay-ley meaning the *home of the fairies*, or Fif and laeh, or Five-Leys meaning *five clearings*. One interesting suggestion was that the name derived from the word 'Fifel' meaning monster or the devil. Fifel-Leah a place haunted by demons. Certainly, the Brigg could be haunted by demons as its treacherous rocks have taken many a ship and many a sailor's life.

At the time this 'great survey' was written, the jurisdiction for the lands attached to Filey was in the manor of *Walesgrif,* (*Falsgrave* as we know it today). This is an extract from the Domesday Book, translated from Latin.

'There are in Walesgrif and in the hamlet of Nordfield 15 geldable (i.e taxable) carucates of land, which will be cultivated by 8 ploughs. (Tosti [brother of King Harold] held these as one manor. Now the King's). There are within this manor 5 villans who hold two carucates. There is wood, with pasturage three miles in length, and two miles in breadth. In the time of King Edward, it was valued at £56.00, now at 30 shillings. To this the manor the jurisdiction of the following lands. Azgodbi (4 carucates) Ledberston, Grieftorp, Scagetorp, Eterstrop, Rodbestrop, Facelac, Bertune, Depedale, Atune, Neuveton, Prestetune, Hortune, Marlane, Wicham, Rosture, Tornelai, Stentun, Brinnistin, Scaltebi, Cloctune.

In the whole, there are 84 carucates of geldable land, which may be cultivated with 42 ploughs. Upon these lands, there were 17 socmen and 15 villans, 14 borders, who have 7 carucates and a half. The rest of the land is waste.'

The Gristhorpe Man

In July 1834, a local landowner William Beswick dug into a barrow on a cliff near Filey. He discovered an ancient British cairn or tumulus. Inside, he exposed intact a perfectly preserved skeleton, which was stained black with the oak tannins. The skeleton was wrapped in an animal skin and surrounded by a drinking-cup, a bronze dagger and flints. The skeleton was a six-foot man who was crushed into a very small space so that his knees nearly touched his chin.

The man had a remarkable muscular physique, he also had a well-developed cranium which showed that he possessed exceptional mental power. The skeleton has since been identified as a Bronze Age warrior chieftain who lived over 4000 years ago, now known worldwide as 'The Gristhorpe Man'. At the time of the discovery, a Mr Gage, who was then the treasurer of the Antiquarian Society supervised the opening of the tumulus. It is reported that the bones were so brittle as to fall to pieces immediately they were exposed to the air and had to be handled carefully.

The skeleton is on view at Rotunda Museum in Scarborough, and was reassessed by Bradford University in 2005, who found that:

'The Gristhorpe Man is one of the tallest men known from the Early Bronze Age in Britain and received a prestigious burial. Isotope analysis of a tooth has indicated he originated from the Scarborough area and ate a lot of meat when he was young. Radiocarbon dating of the tooth dentine has shown that he died around 4000 years ago, (CT scanning of the skull).

The Bradford team analysed the artefacts buried with the body, including metallurgical and isotope analyses of the dagger blade, analysis of the bark container and its contents, a re-assessment of the 'mistletoe berries', and micro-ware on the flint knife. A study of the coffin lid looked at the unique

'face' carved at one end and dendrochronological and radiocarbon dating of the tree rings provided a date for the oak coffin.

In addition, the team carried out geophysical surveys and a small excavation on the site of the original discovery. These have located the 19th-century dig and revealed details of the barrow construction and its preservation. We took pollen samples that enabled us to build up a picture of the local environment at Gristhorpe 4000 years ago,' [2]

Furthermore, towards the end of the nineteenth century, a skeleton of a large deer with magnificent antlers was dug out of the cliffs at Filey. The skeleton was either that of a fallow deer or a red deer. If the former it must have belonged to the glacial period, or if the latter then it would date back to around 500BC. Unfortunately, no records are available to confirm which one it was.

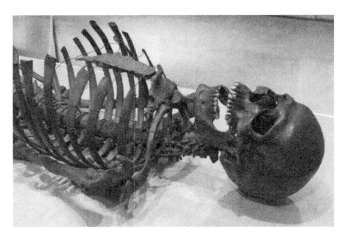

Skeleton of The Gristhorpe Man

2 Bradford University, 2005

Filey Enclosure

An Act of Parliament was passed in 1791, for dividing, allotting, and enclosing the several open and common arable fields, meadows, pastures commons and waste grounds of the township of Filey. Prior to this act, Filey used the Middle Ages system commonly adopted throughout England, whereby land worked by the community was divided into strips. These strips were aggregated into three fields on a rotation system, which allowed each field to lay fallow every 2, 3 or 4 years. These strips were owned or tenanted by the villagers. The division of the strips varied considerably but would be about a furrow long (220 yards) in length and a few yards wide. (Country Park retains clear indications of strip farming as does a part of Glen Gardens.)

Prior to the Enclosure Act; Filey had three fields:

Great Field: The land that now houses Scarborough Road.

Church Field: To the north of St. Oswald's – what is now Country Park.

Little Field: Both sides of what is now West Avenue.

According to working-class politics of the late 18th and 19th centuries, the Enclosure Act stole people's land. The land they had worked for many years. Thus, leaving people impoverished which destroyed the small farmers' agrarian way of life. A life that had sustained families for centuries. Prior to the act English agriculture depended on common land that was privately owned, but to which others enjoyed the right of legal access.

Following this new Act of Parliament, the distribution of land in Filey was carried out by the commissioners appointed by the government. John Dickenson, who was well known as a fair and honest man (he was a Quaker) completed the survey for Filey and concluded that there were

695 Acres, 1 rood, 12 perches (a perch is about 30 square yards.)

In addition to the redistribution of the arable land, the opportunity was taken to widen the main highways i.e. Muston Road, Scarborough Road, Sand Road (Murray Street) Great Carr Goat Road (Ravine Hill) and Cottagers Road (West Road as far as the junior school). Attention was also given to the current drainage system.

The land was allotted as follows:

Humphrey Osbaldeston – 376 acres.

Michael Newton – 122 acres.

Christopher Foster – 101 acres.

Thomas Robinson – 15 acres.

Robert Rowe – 16 acres.

Elizabeth Huntress – 8 acres.

The establishment of clear titles to land was convenient, and a major factor in the ease with which land was acquired for housing of what would later became known as 'New Filey.' (The Crescent)

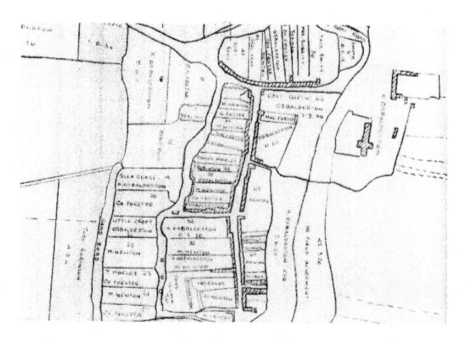

1791 Enclosure Map

Filey Brigg

Credit Stephen Eblet

Filey Brigg or 'Bridge' as it was sometimes known is a rocky peninsula which extends for almost 1.5 km along the north side of Filey Bay and lies 1 km northeast of Filey town. The rocks vary from pure sandstone to limestone and are created by tiny sea creatures invisible to the naked eye. Filey Brigg is universally considered to be a haven for both Geologists and Ornithologists with its fossiliferous rocks and ledges. The Brigg is an ideal place for bird watching, angling, and fossil hunting. Many hours are spent enthusiastically exploring this natural environment, looking for birds such as the Herring Gull, Sand Martins or the Kittiwake.

Credit Stephen Eblet

Partly because of the angle of the strata exposed on the north side of the promontory, the waves have cut out holes in the cliff face. These holes, or shallow caves, are called 'doodles'. They each have a name such as First Doodle, Second Doodle, Long Doodle and Far Doodle. Above water level, there is a layer of hard rock with a softer layer containing 'balls' (hard siliceous masses) above it. Over the years, the waves have washed out these balls, which rolled around eroding away the rock surface beneath them and creating a 'bath'. There are numerous rock pools on the Brigg, including 'The Emperor's Bath', and the treacherous 'Black Hole'. The Black Hole is aptly named as it is far deeper than it looks to the naked eye. It also marks the end of the road for anyone attempting to walk on the seashore to Scarborough.

Emperor's Pool and Fishing on The Brigg

In mid-Victorian times, if as a visitor, you wanted to go on the Brigg, you would be besieged with a dozen boys asking, 'carriage sir, take you to the Brigg for a shilling!' And they would be back to collect you in two hours' time.

Carriages waiting to take visitors to the Brigg

Whilst those days are gone, the one thing that will never change is that the Brigg can be a dangerous place, thus extreme caution should be taken when venturing there, as many areas are slippery, and the cliffs are crumbly, and most importantly, it is imperative that you keep an eye on the incoming tides which can creep up slowly when you least expect it. It is vital to follow the warnings and stay safe. Through the years many people have met their death on the Brigg, even at low tide as the big waves and rough sea-sprays have swept them off their feet. Others not realising the force of the fast-flowing tides are left stranded and trapped and need to be rescued by the Coastguard. Here are a few examples:

In September 1818, twenty-five-year-old William Oddie from Woodlesford, near Leeds was holidaying in Scarborough with two of his friends. They decided to take a boat from Scarborough to Filey. The weather was fine, and they arrived at Filey 'Bridge' shortly after midday. They went ashore and spent an hour or so exploring the rocks and scenery. Then went back to their boat to return to Scarborough. Ten minutes later, a gust of wind plunged the boat underwater – they all clung to the wreck except for Mr Oddie who decided to swim to the shore. However, his heavy overcoat and full-length leather boots encumbered him, thus, he was unable to reach his destination. Panicking, he then decided to turn around and swim back to the boat where his friends were still holding on. When he got within twenty yards of them his hope and stamina waned. With his strength gone, he let out a shriek and disappeared. The other two men were rescued shortly afterwards by a sloop who took them back to Scarborough. Unfortunately, Mr Oddie's body was never recovered.

One of the saddest cases of drowning on the Brigg happened in October 1871, when a Doctor Haworth was shooting birds on the Brigg (how times change) with his two sons and one of their friends. The doctor shot a bird, and his son Joseph climbed onto a rock to reach it when a sudden wave came and washed him into deep water. Although his father was within a few yards of him, he could not reach him. To make matters worse, the family's pet dog, a golden retriever, rushed into the sea to save his master. Unfortunately, the dog placed his paws on Joseph's body which caused him to sink. The poor boy's body was recovered shortly afterwards by local fishermen.

In a secluded commemorative corner of Filey Parish churchyard (St Oswald's) and graced by weeping willows marks a small cross, which serves as a memorial to twelve sailors who in January 1871 far away from their homeland and their loved ones, lost their lives. They drowned at sea when a coal-laden Italian Barque named *The Unico* which was heading between Newcastle and Constantinople struck violently against the rocks on Filey Brigg, the vessel shattered on impact. Only the captain from a crew of thirteen survived. This and similar tragedies of the time raised the question of the need for a Harbour of Refuge to be built at Filey, which would help to prevent similar disasters to that of the ill-fated *Unico*.

Agony Point

In 1873, Mr Paget the retired MP for Nottinghamshire and his wife Ellen tragically drowned as they stood on a ledge close to 'Emperor's Bath' when an exceptionally large wave washed them into the sea and they were never seen again. In memory of the couple, their family erected a memorial stone on the Brigg, which was intended as a warning to others. This stone is now on display in Filey Museum. Fifty years later at the same spot, Mr Albert Shakesby, a primitive Methodist evangelist, rescued a young lady visitor who later said, 'I owe my life to him; he is a brave man.'

Agony Point showing the plaque erected by the Paget family to warn others of the dangers of the Brigg

IN MEMORY OF
CHARLES PAGET, Esq., of Ruddington Grange, Notts., J.P.
FORMERLY M.P. FOR NOTTINGHAM, AND OF ELLEN, HIS WIFE WHO WERE SWEPT OFF
FILEY ROCKS, BY A WAVE OF EXTRAORDINARY VOLUME AND DROWNED
ON THE 13TH OF OCTOBER, 1873.

AT THE TIME OF THE FATAL OCCURRENCE THEY WERE STANDING ON THE ROCKS
NEAR THE SECOND CAVE, WHERE THEY HAD BEEN IN SAFETY FOR MORE
THAN A QUARTER OF AN HOUR. THE SPOT IN QUESTION IS RARELY COVERED AT
HIGH TIDE, AND AT THE TIME IT ONLY WANTED AN HOUR
AND A HALF TO LOW WATER.

THIS SLAB IS PLACED HERE BY THE MEMBERS OF THE FAMILY, TO WARN OTHERS
AGAINST THE DANGER OF VENTURING ON THE ROCKS DURING
HEAVY GROUND SWELL.

Searching for the bodies 1873

The Wreck of The Chilean 1894

The Wreck of The Chilean 1894

In 1894, a steamer named the *Chilean*, a new vessel belonging to The Grimsby Incorporated Box Fishing Company (Limited) was on its way back to its homeport of Grimsby, after a journey to Iceland. It was just heading into Filey Bay when dense fog prevented the steamer's Captain Little from knowing his exact whereabouts, (by all accounts there had been problems with the vessel's compass instrument). Captain Little ordered the engineers full steam astern but found that the vessel would not come off. He blew the whistle with one long blast until he had no choice but to attempt to save himself and his crew.

Twenty minutes later the vessel crashed onto Filey Brigg. The vessel was steering south-east, and there was a light breeze blowing in the same direction. Captain Little sent a warning of the dangers that lay ahead to the steam-trawler that was following his pilotage, averting a second disaster the captain then grabbed a life jacket and he told his crew to take to the rigging, but only he and four others did so. Four hours passed before a trawler came and saved them.

Six of the other crew who attempted to launch the small boat was washed away by the heavy waves that crashed over the boat and onto the Brigg. The body of one man, which was found on the deck was taken to T'Oard' Ship Inn in Queen Street Filey, where he was identified as Charles Barker from Scarborough.

A few feet away from the Brigg a well-known bell-buoy would be tolling at the time the vessel struck, but the noise of the breakers prevented any warning to the steamer. Furthermore, the gun at Flamborough Head, which is sounded every five minutes in foggy weather, also failed to warn the steamer of its proximity to the rocks.

Credit Ian Nisbet

Filey Brigg Offered For Sale

FILEY BRIGG

Famous Promontory for Sale

PURCHASER WOULD HAVE POWER TO FENCE IT

Public's Rights Would Be Safeguarded

Scarborough Mercury 1931

Today it is inconceivable for us to consider that the Brigg was once privately owned. However, it only became freely accessible to the public in 1955. Prior to this, the Brigg was owned by the Lord of The Manor of Filey, and the owner of Hunmanby Hall and Estates who had manorial rites over the Brigg and a part of the foreshore.

Ancient manorial rights in England date back to the Norman Conquest, whereby manorialism was characterised by vesting powers in the Lord of the manor. This right was given by William the Conqueror to Gilbert de Gant the Manor of Hunmanby, which became one of the most powerful manors in the North of England. Gilbert's son William founded Bridlington Priory, which was built with some of the stone from Filey Brigg.

The manor changed hands many times throughout the centuries but retained its manorial importance until the end of the nineteenth century when the hereditary Lord of the Manor sold the estate to the High

Sheriff of Yorkshire Sir Dennis Readett Dennis-Bayley a Nottinghamshire Coal Mine owner, who in 1925/6 sold the land piece by piece to his tenants. As the owner of Hunmanby estates, and thus The Lord of The Manor of Filey he was entitled to exercise his ancient manorial rights and perform a 'Patrol of the Brigg', a ceremony performed every three or four years and for many years previously. This rite consisted of dragging a net around the sea-line of the Brigg and gathering fish which were then distributed, an assistant to the Lord would then mount a horse and ride over the Brigg as far as the low-water mark.

Sir Readett-Bayley took his role very seriously as in 1930, he wrote to Filey Urban District Council to complain about 'unauthorised people using the sands on his land for the exercising of their horses (riding school) and that he intended to take steps to prevent them!' The council replied that this was not a matter that they could interfere in. Sir Readett-Bayley also pointed out that the owners of the adjoining land owned the property up to the high-water mark and that the board of trade and Filey Town council have certain rights and that the long uninterrupted usage by the public was a factor to be taken into consideration.

In March 1931, an advertisement appeared in the press that Sir Readett-Bayley had offered for sale Filey Brigg, part of the foreshore and manorial and mineral rights to this. The advertisement (Yorkshire Post/Leeds Intelligencer/Scarborough Mercury) stipulated that the Lord of the Manor was prepared to sell as two lots either the Brigg only or The Brigg with the foreshore and mineral rights. Furthermore, the advert stated that the purchaser will control an area of about a mile and a half, and on another a quarter of a mile.

Perhaps, Sir Readett-Bayley was calling Filey Urban District Council's bluff, but they responded accordingly stating that 'if the Brigg were to pass into private ownership-and an attempt made to exclude the public then the council would have a duty to the public to intervene and safeguard any rights, by way of a passage over any private properties.

However, prior to the onslaught of the second world war, a proposal was put forward to Filey Urban District Council by a Leeds based syndicate for substantial development of 320 acres of land belonging to The Church Cliff Estate, between the Brigg and Church Ravine and beyond. Mr Tom Smith the owner of Church Cliff Farm discussed the intentions of the syndicate which were to build a first-class housing estate, shops, a large hotel, concert hall and a cinema. He also indicated that included within this sale was Carr Naze, but it could include the Brigg and part of the Foreshore (still in the ownership of Sir Readett-Bayley) subject to negotiation, and the proposal included developing this area and that the syndicate would provide a life from the cliffs to the beach and build a promenade from the beach to the Brigg.

Mr W Bramham, another syndicate member stated that pending a few minor details the purchase was completed and proposed that the priority was to build three-hundred quality houses on the land, expressing that a development of this type would be beneficial for Filey as a town. Filey Urban District Council approved all the plans and were in favour of the development, but the purchase did not go ahead and plans shelved until after the war.

FILEY, YORKSHIRE.
JOSEPH CUNDALL and SONS will offer for
Sale by Auction, unless previously sold by
Private Treaty, and subject to Conditions of
Sale, at the THREE TUNS HOTEL, FILEY, on
FRIDAY, 29th SEPTEMBER, at 3 p.m.
precisely.
The VALUABLE FREEHOLD BUILDING and
AGRICULTURAL PROPERTY
known as

CHURCH CLIFF FARM,

FILEY, containing 320.459 ACRES or thereabouts, situate in a commanding position
adjoining the Ravine and the shore of Filey
Bay, and lying in a ring fence extending to
Filey Brigg, together with the SUPERIOR
RESIDENCE and EXTENSIVE RANGE OF
FARM BUILDINGS.
The property has a sea frontage of about
two miles and long road frontage to the Scar-
borough Road, and it is believed that future
development will include a substantial part
if not the whole of the land, a good deal of
which is potential building land.
Further particulars and Permission to View
may be obtained from the Auctioneers, Sherburn,
Malton, Yorks, or from the Solicitors, Messrs.
LAMBERT and PARKINSON, Bridlington and
Filey.

Advert Yorkshire Post/Leeds Intelligencer 1944

In 1944, following the war Church Cliff Farm sold 320 acres of land for
£24,500 to a Mr Taylor of Driffield. When asked what he thought
would be best done with this substantial amount of land Mr Taylor
responded that he had bought the land specifically for speculation
purposes and that his intention foremost was to make money.
However, he liked Filey and wanted the best development possible for
the town. He was, however, shocked that the council were not in
favour of his plans and objected to him building houses within 100 feet
of the coastline which were spectacular views.

Despite, planning approval agreed before the war the new Town and Country Planning Act empowered authorities to revoke previous development approvals and query decisions. This is exactly what Filey Urban District Council did.

Mr Taylor was not at all happy with this decision and argued the matter at an enquiry stating that he was prepared to offer land to the Council on Carr Naze to build a war memorial, but if they wanted any more land they would have to buy it off him at a reasonable price of no less than £5,000.

Filey Council and Mr Taylor were at loggerheads with neither side talking to each other only via solicitors.

Wisely, the decision was reached in favour of the Town Council the ministry deciding to refuse Mr Taylor's planning application not to allow building so near to Carr Naze on the north-east of the town in the public interests of the town. Later, new plans were submitted and a much-needed housing estate was built.

Five years later, an announcement was made in the Yorkshire Post/Leeds Intelligencer by Mr Kenneth Henderson of Filey Council that under the Public Health Act 1875, it had entered into private negotiations with representatives of the late Sir Henry Readett-Bayley (he died in 1940) to purchase the Brigg for the benefit of the people of Filey and to retain it for public use, an agreement was reached and the Brigg purchased for the sum of £250. This was the first time in its history that the Brigg had not been in private ownership. The council now owned all their sea-boundaries districts and have been enjoyed freely by many people ever since.

A Cafe on The Brigg

The Original Cafe on the Brigg

A welcome sight for thirsty travellers was a cafe on the Brigg, unfortunately, in March 1906, a severe storm ravaged the town of Filey and the cafe and its contents were completely swept away by the high tides. The Vicar of Filey Canon Cooper started a charity to replace the cafe on account of its owner losing his entire life savings.

The New Cafe built after the Storm of 1906

Spittal Rocks

On the south side of Filey Brigg is a rocky peninsula known as The Spittals. For many years' there has been speculation as to whether this is a natural or a man-made structure? Some say that this spectacular structure is the remains of an ancient Roman road, or possibly a harbour, while others say that it was most likely constructed for the transportation of stone from the Brigg across the water to build Bridlington Priory. This splendid structure is 600 meters long and thirty paces wide. Records show that over the year's fishermen have seen old iron mooring rings exposed at the exceptionally low tide. Also, when the tide is very low, some rare kinds of anemones may be found in the crevices beneath the layers of rocks, near the water's edge. The Spittals are not accessible except at spring tides when they offer a rich reward for the naturalist seeking treasure.

Monsters and Dragons

In 1857, Mr Ruddock of Filey discovered what was described as 'A Monster of the Deep' an oceanic creature that had washed up on the beach a half-mile from the sea-wall parade. This 'monster' was 33 feet long had fins and ten feet and weighed twenty pounds. Later in 1934 there were several sightings of monsters spotted off Filey Brigg which created quite a sensation. Reports varied some saying that the monster had 'eyes like saucers, humps, scales and a large body.' One report stated that a man walking on the Brigg had seen a monster in the sea with a small head and lots of humps. On further investigation, it was found to be a school of porpoises in a row.

On another occasion fishermen thought they saw a large sea-monster two-miles offshore, they rushed to get a better view, where they found a large seal basking on the rocks.

To this day reports come in of strange 'monsters' seen in the sea around Filey, who knows perhaps one day the real monster may just reveal itself?

Spa Well

FILEY SPA WELL.

Spa Well the Summer House in the background

During the early nineteenth century taking the waters was a Victorian passion around the country. Spa towns flourished and Filey was no exception and offered its own contribution to the development of the town as a seaside resort, by supplying visitors with its own invigorating health cure in the form of 'healing spa water.'

The spa, which no longer exists, was centred upon a small spring alleged to have healing qualities. It was located on the north side of Carr-Naze and was not a place to seek out for the faint-hearted, as it was situated close to the edge, and a step in the wrong direction could have fatal consequences. To reach the spa, visitors had to walk about a quarter of a mile from North Coble Landing across the beach, then onto the Brigg where steps led to the spa well. It is here where visitors first encountered the running water. This projection was well named as 'agony point'. In 1844, Dr William Cortis persuaded the then owner of the land Miss Brooke, of Selby to open the Spa to the public. Prior to his intervention, the Spa was virtually unknown. The area was full of weeds and rubbish and extremely difficult to find. Dr Cortis suggested, that the well is made more accessible, with a good road formed up to it. Taking the doctors' advice, a summerhouse was erected to allow visitors to take in the views through the season. For some years, Miss Brooke collected subscriptions from the public, which she used to employ an attendant to dispense the water. Two eminent specialists, namely Professor Fyfe of Edinburgh, and Mr West of Leeds had analysed the water and found that it possessed valuable medicinal properties. An unknown visitor dedicated this poem to Miss Brooke as a thank you for making the 'Spa Well' available to the public.

On the Renovation of Filey Spa

A blessing meets us here this hill

Gives from its brow a trickling rill

With healing virtues, rife

In rude neglect t'was long concealed

Now, to the public gaze revealed

Its waters oft' may prove a well of life

Thanks to the lady who kind thought

I was to such a pleasing beauty wrought

The birthplace of this spring

She wound a pathway to this spot

She rear'd the cool umbrageous grot

Where grandeur hovers around on breezy wing

But let our highest thanks be given

To him, who from his throne in heaven

Regards, all human wants

He bids to elevate the soul

The mighty waves of ocean roll

And for the body's health this well-spring grants

The notorious Dr Edward William Pritchard reiterated this claim in his book *A Guide to Filey* claiming that 'taking the waters has significant gains for your health in that the medicinal values of this water are efficacious in the treatment of dyspepsia, scrofula, and nervous diseases.' He also claimed that the water contained magnesium, calcium and soda, with a small quantity of iron, iodine and bromine. 'Which are all beneficial for one's health and help maintain the body's equilibrium.' However, it was later claimed that any health-giving properties of the waters were dubious and over-exaggerated, proposing that the spa waters were even a cure for chronic rheumatism, and a miraculous cure for most general nervous conditions, together with ailments of a 'scrupulous or scorbutic nature'.

Miss Brook died in 1869, and the property changed hands. Consequently, a dispute arose over access to the right of way to the Spa, which was on privately owned land. This dispute resulted in the Spa being boarded off. The Spa, like many others around the country, fell from favour, with the advent of more trusted and easily available medicines. After the closure of the Spa, a Victorian graffiti was found inscribed on the boarding.

Though boarded up

It still flows out

Drink for dyspepsia

Or for gout

In 1951, a project was launched for the Festival of Britain year, and members of a Filey local History Group spent a lot of time and effort restoring the site, but unfortunately, coastal erosion has removed all the remains of the Spa, which has since slipped down the cliff and into the sea.

John Paul Jones and the Battle of the Bonhomme Richard

JOHN PAUL JONES.

The Battle of *The Bonhomme Richard* was fought off Filey Bay in September 1779 and has for generations been described as a memorable and intense battle, resulting in the events still being discussed over two centuries later. The central character of the story is Captain John Paul Jones, a man who has attracted the attention of two continents, and who in his brief career has received eternal fame among the heroes of the world.

John Paul (he added the Jones later, in tribute to his close friend and active American Revolutionary leader Willie Jones) was born of humble origin on the 6th July 1747, in Kirkcudbrightshire, Scotland. He was the fourth child of seven children. His father was John Paul Snr a gardener for the Earl of Selkirk. His mother was Jean McDuff (part of the McDuff clan). Neither of his parents registered their son's birth.

Living close to the sea, Jones soon developed a spirit for seafaring and adventure. At the age of twelve, the young John Paul ran away to sea and signed up for a seven-year seaman's apprenticeship. His first voyage took him to Barbados and Fredericksburg in Virginia where he spent time learning navigation.

He soon adopted America as his native country and considered England his enemy. In 1768, he participated in the transportation of slaves in ships that were totally unfit for humans. He soon quit making his fortune as a merchant seaman. Soon after, he was arrested for the alleged murder of a crew member who he ordered to be flogged. Jones later produced evidence to show that the man died, not from his wounds, but from yellow fever whilst on another ship.

Cleared of those charges, he was embroiled in a second scandal when he ran his broadsword through a sailor. According to a letter written years later to Benjamin Franklin, Jones was forced to defend himself against the ringleader of a mutinous crew while in the West Indies. He wrote that he considered this incident to be the 'greatest misfortune of my life.' By his account, he immediately rowed ashore to the island of Tobago to turn himself into the Justice of the Peace. However, his friends advised him to leave his accumulated fortune behind him and flee to America, which he did before there was time for him to stand trial.

John Paul was still poor, and obscure when he arrived in the colonies in 1774, where he then took the name John Paul Jones. Fortunately for him, he was in the right place at the right time and he quickly climbed the ranks within America's plight for independence. He wrote to Joseph Hewes (the man who signed America's Declaration of Independence) to ask him personally, for a naval appointment. In December 1775, he was appointed as a First Lieutenant in the Navy.

The American War of Independence was an armed conflict between Great Britain and thirteen of its former North American colonies. The conflict took place during the years 1775-1783, with the Declaration of Independence being issued on 4th July 1776. Relations between Britain and her American colonies had deteriorated following a British attempt to make the colonies contribute to the cost of their own defence, and those opposing this wanted to break free from constraints imposed by the British aristocracy. Fundamentalists, and radical politicians such as Sam Adams and Paul Revere, encouraged a break with Britain, whilst others hoped that this drastic action would be avoided.

The descent into armed conflict between patriot (anti-British) and loyalist (pro-British) sympathisers was gradual. Events such as the Boston 'Massacre' of 1770, when British troops fired on a mob that had attacked a British sentry outside Boston's State House, and the Boston 'tea-party' of 1773, when British-taxed tea was thrown into the harbour, were key turning points. Less obvious was the take-over of the colonial militias, which had initially been formed to defend against the French and the Native Americans. These units were run by officers in sympathy with the American patriots/rebels, rather than by soldiers in sympathy with pro-British loyalists. After initial clashes during 1775, the British landed 30,000 troops near New York in the summer of 1776 under General Howe. The city was taken, and the war began in earnest.

Jones was appointed as a 1st Lieutenant of the 24-gun frigate USS *Alfred* a small converted merchantman in the newly founded Continental Navy on 7th December 1775. The flagship of Commodore Hopkins. It was on this ship that he had the honour to become the first man to raise 'The Grand Union Liberty Flag'. There is also controversy as to whether this was the stars and stripes flag or the famous yellow silk banner with a rattlesnake, and perhaps a pine tree, emblazoned upon it, with the significant legend. 'Don't tread on me!'

Credit US Bonhomme Richard (January 2017)

He later captained '*The Ranger*', and in 1778, Jones and his crew crossed the Solway Frith from Whitehaven to Scotland, this time hoping to take for ransom the Earl of Selkirk (the very man his father had worked for). Jones' intention was to kidnap him and exchange him for American sailors who had been *impressed* into the Royal Navy. However, The Earl was not at home, only the Countess and her young family. Instead, Jones and his crew made off with the silverware from the estate. Jones continued his journey raiding Whitehaven on the north-west coast of England and seeing action in Ireland and Scotland (earning the reputation of a 'pirate' in Britain), before taking charge of the 44-gun USS *Bonhomme Richard* in 1779.

The *Bonhomme Richard* was an aged East Indiaman. Originally built in 1765 it was formerly named *Duc de Duras*, a merchant ship built for the French East India Co, for service between France and the Orient. The ship was placed at the disposal of John Paul Jones on 4th February 1779, by King Louis XVI of France because of a loan to the United States by French shipping magnate, Jacques-Donatien Le Ray de Chaumont, who historians consider to be the 'Father of the American Revolution'. As a compliment to Benjamin Franklin's almanack '*Poor Richard*' the ship was renamed *The Bonhomme Richard* (Good Man Richard). At the time that Jones took her command, the ship had already had four gruelling voyages to the Far East and back. This was not the type of ship Jones was expecting, having already declared 'I will have no connection with any ship that does not sail fast, for I intend to go in harm's way.'

Initially, the *Duc de Duras* was designed as a two-decker with 32 guns, with two-gun decks which ran from bow to stern. However, Jones later adapted the ship to suit his needs. Jones hand-picked his crew, and per a letter printed in *The London Chronicle* of the 28th September 1779 it states that most of Jones' crew were English and Irish, many of them taken out of prisons at Brest and St. Malo. At that time, prisoners were offered their liberty on condition that they serve on Jones' fleet. However, they were treated as prisoners whilst on board. The article quotes: 'There were few Americans, some French and some neutrals, such as Dutch and Germans'.

Captain Richard Pearson took a commission of *The Serapis* on 8th March 1779. Captain Richard Pearson was born in Appleby, Westmoreland in 1731. He entered the Navy in 1745 aged fourteen. Pearson was a Lieutenant during the Seven Years' War where he was very successful but was himself badly wounded in the conflict. Pearson finally received his commission as Captain in January 1773. *The Serapis* was launched from Deptford Dockyard in March the same year. Named after the Greek God of fertility and the afterlife, *The Serapis* is described as having been an exceedingly fine ship with good sailing properties. *The Serapis* was rated a 44-gun ship and mounted her guns on two complete decks. The present complement of the class was a trained man-of-war's crew of two hundred and eighty-five men.

The Serapis at Sea

Jones' orders were simple. He was instructed to 'burn, sink or destroy all'. *The Bonhomme Richard*, together with four smaller vessels, *The Alliance, The Pallas, The Cerf*, and *The Vengeance*, of which only *The Alliance* and *The Cerf* were properly fitted for war, set sail from L'Orient on 19th June 1779, striking terror on their journey.

On 23rd September 1779 while *The Serapis* and *The Countess of Scarborough* were anchored under Scarborough Castle. Captain Pearson received intelligence that Jones and his American convoy were in Burlington Bay (Bridlington), which was a few leagues windward. The English ships departed keeping a watchful eye out for the American convoy and its notorious Commodore John Paul Jones. Around six in the evening, it was all hands to quarters, as four vessels came into sight. *The Serapis* made the signal to *The Countess of Scarborough* to stay close to their stern. English colours were hoisted on both ships.

The wind was slight that evening as the American ships came up very slowly. Captain Pearson instructed that the ports in the lower deck were to be down. This was meant as a decoy. However, the enemy was far too cunning and soon saw through this. At about seven-thirty, the enemy ships bore close and hoisted American colours, but it was so dark that they were presumed to be the colours of St. George, and orders were given on pain of death not to fire. To be certain, Captain Pearson hailed her, and believed the response to be *'Princess Amelia.'* He hailed again with the warning: 'If you do not tell us clearly from whence you came we will fire you (now they were very close, within half a pistol shot, but it was too dark to recognise their colours). Suddenly, there was a flash of gunfire in one of the lower decks, *The Serapis* responded instantaneously by giving them a broadside. Initially, it was clear that *The Serapis* had superior firepower. However, John Paul Jones chose to fight at close range to overcome his disadvantage. The ships were so close that the nozzles of the guns touched as the vessels rolled on heavy seas. There was no time to be lost, the enemy was all too close, every shot told, and only a few yards' distance. There was no choice but to haul the dead and wounded from the guns and to fire and load at the same time.

By this time, a huge crowd of people had gathered on the cliffs and on the shore to watch the battle by the light of the rising moon. Some of the gunfire was so near that a few cannon-balls grazed Flamborough's white cliffs. For the next two hours firing continued, with many deaths on both sides with people jumping ships to save themselves, Jones managed to carry away the jib-boom from *The Serapis* (to ensure they would not sail off too far). *The Bonhomme Richard's* bow and *The Serapis* touched, and as fast as they could each raise guns, shots were fired.

Gradually, *The Serapis* shot away the entire side of *The Bonhomme Richard*, which was riddled like a sieve, causing the ship to take in several feet of water in the hold. Her rotten sides were almost blown out to starboard and port by the batteries of *The Serapis*. Captain Pearson was a brave man, but he was no match for the indomitable personality of the American Commander. After several hours of fighting, he asked Jones if he wanted to strike (surrender) to which Jones famously replied, 'I have not yet begun to fight.' Reports state that unlike the honourable Captain Pearson, Jones would have sunk the ship, men, and himself, before he would have 'struck.' When told that *The Bonhomme Richard* was sinking Jones said, 'let her sink and be damned, she cannot be in a better place than alongside an English man-of-war!' Some of Jones' crew cried out 'we have struck' and *The Serapis* Boatswain went on board *The Bonhomme Richard* to take possession of her, he was met with a Frenchman's small sword in his groin, and another through his brain, he fell back onto *The Serapis* where he died instantly.

The Bonhomme Richard's damaged gun decks were barely capable of fighting, it was a terrible scene, there were dead lying on the living, there were men without arms, men without legs, many bleeding to death as there were no dressings as two of the three doctors were dead, besides there were no dressings left. Yet still, with Jones' leadership and determination, the remaining crew fought on through the night.

Gun Deck onboard The Bonhomme Richard

As the water rose in *The Bonhomme Richard* fear set into the mind of John Burbank her master-at-arms, consequently, he took pity on the crying prisoners who were trapped in the hole with water rising around them, so without orders, Burbank opened the hatches and released the British prisoners caught in previous actions. Jones was furious, and instantly put them to work manning the sinking ship's water pumps. These prisoners were terrified but grateful to have been set free. They could have quite easily tipped the balance against the Americans, and they could have all bolted and jumped ship, shot Jones or thrown him overboard, but surprisingly most of them stayed put. Perhaps they were more concerned with saving themselves from imminent drowning or shot on the spot, but because of their actions, they became an integral part of the subsequent American victory.

However, a few did escape taking advantage of the confusion and made their escape to Filey, where they were made prisoner and taken before Humphrey Osbaldeston, Hunmanby.

Conflict on The Bonhomme Richard

Once again Captain Pearson called Jones to strike, or you must infallibly sink to the bottom. Jones replied, 'I may sink, but I'll be damned if I strike!' At this time one of Jones' crew attempted to strike the colours but Jones turned around and shot him dead on the spot, another two attempted and suffered the same fate. A mutiny was expected to take place as the ship was sinking when one of Jones' squadron immediately came to his assistance which turned the tables on *The Serapis*. *The Bonhomme Richard* was in such a bad way. The rudder was gone, the stern frame and stanchions were cut away, the timbers of the lower deck from the mainmast to stern were mangled beyond description, dying men were lying in pools of blood and groaning piteously. The ship was burning in several places, and the water in the hold was rising steadily. Realising that *The Bonhomme Richard* was sinking and the seriousness of the situation, Jones still fought doggedly on, until the mizzenmast of *The Serapis* went by the board, whereupon Captain Pearson called for quarter, and Jones then ordered a boarding crew onto *The Serapis,* and against all odds captured *The Serapis* and its crew, where they triumphantly raised their country's colours. *The Countess of Scarborough* suffered a similar fate as she surrendered to *The Pallas* and *The Alliance.*

Many lives were lost on both sides of the conflict. This is an account of the ships men, and guns prior to engagement.

The American's Capt. Jones	Guns	Men
Bonhomme Richard - Jones	44	380
Pallas-Cpt Cottineau	32	320
Alliance-Cpt Landais	36	300
Vengeance	12	100
TOTAL	124	1100
THE ENGLISH	Guns	Men
The Serapis-Cpt-Pearson	44	285
The Countess of Scarborough	20	100
TOTAL	64	385

Therefore, it was clear that from the beginning of the battle Jones had three times more men than the English (715) and 60 more guns.

Accounts from the time show that the loss of life on both sides was horrendous and as follows:

The Bonhomme Richard – 250 men killed and wounded.

The Pallas – 6 men and 1 Lieutenant killed, with many wounded.

The Alliance – Nobody killed - 2 wounded.

The English

The Serapis – 125 killed and wounded.

The Countess of Scarborough – 30 killed and wounded.

Total loss of life on both sides: 411.

Two days later between the hours of ten and eleven on the morning of 25th September, *The Bonhomme Richard* drifted towards Filey Bay where she eventually sank, her flag flying as she went down. Nothing of her was saved except her signal flag. John Paul Jones and his victorious crew and prizes sailed *The Serapis and The Countess of Scarborough* along with Captain Pearson and his crew as hostages to Texel in the Netherlands where Jones sought safe harbour and where the ship received much-needed repairs.

The Serapis was the first British vessel ever to be captured by an American ship, causing British fears of an invasion and a fleet being dispatched from across the Atlantic. The English were exasperated at the humiliation suffered by the total defeat of one of their best frigates. Sir Joseph Yorke, British Ambassador, wrote to the Dutch on behalf of the King of England to protest at Jones' conduct saying that, '*The Serapis* and *The Countess of Scarborough* and their Captains and crew were attacked and taken by force by John Paul Jones who had received no commission from his own country. Therefore, to the treaties and laws of war, he falls under the classification of Rebels and Pirates.' The Dutch did not agree to the Ambassador's request, stating that they would prefer to 'observe neutrality.' On 7th October, Jones left the ship and went to Amsterdam. Captain Pearson was kept as a hostage and finally released on 21st November 1779 in exchange for Captain Gustave Conyngham, whom the British were holding prisoner.

Captain Jones was not at all happy with John Burbank the master-at-arms on *The Bonhomme Richard* and he insisted that he be put in irons for liberating prisoners during the conflict.

On 3rd October 1870, Captain Pearson was honourably acquitted by a Court Martial for the loss of *The Serapis* and was instead knighted by the

King of England for his services to this most famous battle. When Jones was told of this, he is reported to have said: 'Never mind, if I meet him again, I'll make a Lord of him!' Captain Pearson died in 1806 at The Royal Naval Hospital in Greenwich, where he was Lieutenant Governor.

The Serapis was on loan to Benjamin Franklin to aid the American Revolution, the French ordered Captain Cottineau de Kerlogeun to take command of *The Serapis* in the Texel and bring her back to France. Subsequently, *The Serapis* was refitted for the French Navy and under Captain Roche sent to assist in a campaign to wrest India from British rule. Roche proceeded to the French fort, Île Sainte-Marie located off the northern coast of Madagascar. While Roche was ashore, a lieutenant and a subordinate went below deck to obtain the daily brandy ration for the sailors. While the men were 'cutting' the brandy's full strength with water, their lantern fell into the vat and set the spirit locker on fire. Attempts to extinguish the blaze failed and after two-and-a-half hours, the flames burned through the locker walls and reached the powder magazine. An explosion blew out the stern and the vessel sank.

Like the wreck of *The Bonhomme Richard*, the whereabouts of *The Serapis* was for many years unknown. However, in November 1999 it was discovered by American nautical archaeologist, Richard Swete and his associate Michael Tuttle. After many years of research and a systematic magnetometer survey of the harbour on Île Sainte-Marie, Swete and a team of archaeologists finally discovered the remains of *The Serapis*.

Despite being venerated today; John Paul Jones was never promoted to a rank higher than that of Captain in the American Navy. Strangely enough, he did become an admiral in 1788. However, ironically it was in Russia's Black Sea fleet, at the invitation of Empress Catherine II. He was also appointed US Consul to Algiers in 1792, but he never got the chance to take up this position, as on 18th July 1792, John Paul Jones was found dead face down on his bed at his residence at Rue de Tournon Paris. He was forty-five years old. The cause of death was kidney failure.

John Paul Jones was buried in Paris at the Saint Louis Cemetery, which belonged to the French royal family. Four years later, France's revolutionary government sold the property and the cemetery was forgotten. Jones's body was preserved in alcohol and interred in a lead coffin 'in the event that should the United States decide to claim his remains, they might more easily be identified.' After a lengthy search, Jones' body was taken back to America.

On 24th April 1906, Jones' coffin was installed in Bancroft Hall at the United States Naval Academy, Annapolis, Maryland. On 26th January 1913, the Captain's remains were finally re-interred in a magnificent bronze and marble casket at the Naval Academy Chapel in Annapolis. John Paul Jones is considered to be the father of The American Navy.

To this day, the search for the wreckage of *The Bonhomme Richard* continues. This cannot be an easy task. After all, this was an ageing ship (it was 14 years old before it sank) that has been at the bottom of the sea for over two hundred and thirty years. Furthermore, it was constructed of timber and badly damaged and on fire prior to sinking. If located it would be a tremendous find for the American's and a boost to tourism in the area, putting Filey and the Yorkshire Coast firmly at the centre of American history, and an integral part of its fight for Independence.

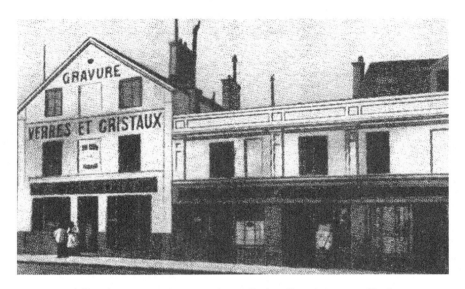

The house in Paris where John Paul Jones died

Sir Captain Richard Pearson

In a letter dated 14th October 1779 Captain Richard Pearson gives his account of the battle, in which he states:

'On my going on board *The Bonhomme Richard*. I found her in great distress, her quarters and counter on the lower deck entirely drove in, and the whole of her lower decks dismounted, she was also on fire in two places with six or seven feet of water in her hold which increased throughout the night and into the next day until we were obliged to quit her, and she sank, with a great number of wounded people on board her. She had 306 men killed and wounded in the action. I am extremely sorry for losing his majesty's ship that I had the honour to command, but at the same time, I flatter myself with the hopes, that their Lordships will be convinced that she has not been given away, but on the contrary, that every exertion has been used to defend her, and that two essential pieces of service to our country has arisen from it. The one is wholly oversetting the crews of this flying squadron, the other is referring the whole of a valuable convoy into the hands of the enemy, which I believe would have been the case had I acted other than the way I did.'

Filey Harbour of Refuge

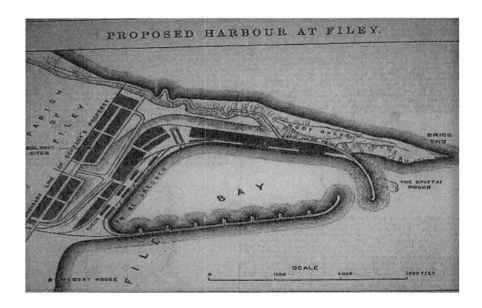

For many years, there had been proposals for the building of a Harbour in Filey. The reasons were threefold. Firstly, numerous lives were lost at sea each year due to adverse weather conditions, and a harbour would be a safe place of refuge for sailing ships. Secondly, the import and export of general cargo, and thirdly, for a place to land fish and maintain vessels.

In 1858, Prime minister Viscount Palmerston set up a Royal select committee to report on the most advantageous places for forming

Harbours of Refuge along the coast of England. Subsequently, a panel of seven 'experts' including sea captains and Royal Navy engineers were elected who were expected to be 'competent and impartial'. The sites in question were Wick, Peterhead, The Tyne, Hartlepool, St. Ives, Padstow, Isle of Man and Filey.

In support of a harbour at Filey Civil Engineer John Coode presented detailed proposals to Parliament with over 3,000 signatures from masters, mates and seamen, regarding the possibility of building a harbour of refuge in Filey Bay. The estimated cost of the proposed harbour was £860,000. The petition recorded:

'For many centuries, large numbers of vessels had been detained off Flamborough Head by southerly winds. Under these circumstances vessels will constantly run in and bring up in the south part of Filey Bay, off Speeton and Bempton cliffs, where they will not uncommonly lay for a week … last month there were at one time not less than 240 vessels so anchored in the south part of Filey Bay.'

In 1860, after a thorough investigation of all the proposed areas, the commission concluded that a saving of eight hundred lives and one million pounds in property could be saved on the country's shores each year. Therefore, the report earnestly recommended that Filey should be made a national harbour of refuge entirely at the expense of the public. And for this purpose, the commission recommended the largest grant ever given to any public place in the three kingdoms of eight hundred thousand pounds.

The select committee submitted its report and advised that harbours around the coast were to be constructed and awarded the following grants:

Filey	£800,000
Hartlepool	£500,000
St. Ives	£400,000

The Tyne	**£250,000**
The Isle of Man	**£140,000**
Wick	**£125,000**
Peterhead	**£100,000**
Padstow	**£40,000**

Proposed Harbour of Refuge. Credit Stephen Eblet

However, despite the competent and impartial views of the select committee and Mr Coode's industrious research and the strength of his evidence supporting the project, nothing came of this scheme. It seems that the project was simply too expensive. In 1866, an eminent government officer is reported to have said: 'It is not the duty of Government to care for the lives and property of merchant seamen.' Therefore, the whole expensive inquiry was deemed useless and the government scheme was abandoned.

Unperturbed, the people of Filey were determined that a harbour would be built, so in December 1863 a company was formed to construct a pier and harbour on a smaller scale as first recommended by the select committee. The company was called *The Filey Harbour Company*. Its distinguished directors were:

General Sir J M Frederick Smith (who was a part of the government select committee).

The Right Hon James Meek, Lord Mayor of York.

Henry Bentley, Ravine Hall, Filey.

George Beswick Esq, Muston Lodge, Filey.

C.W Faber, Director of Great Northern Railway.

J Kitson, Director Great Northern Railway.

George Salt Esq, Saltaire, Bradford.

John Unett Esq, Birmingham & Filey.

William S Cortis Esq, Engineer, Filey.

John Coode Esq, Engineer, London.

The company's intention was to build and maintain a harbour, with piers, jetties, landing places, breakwaters, roads and all other conveniences connected therein. There would be a quay or a pier which would commence approximately 70 yards southward of a point on the western shore of Filey Bay to be called 'North Coble Landing' and extending seawards 1130 yards in an easterly direction. A breakwater commencing near to the eastern extremity of Carr Naze point on the northern side of Filey Bay and extending along Filey Brigg in an easterly direction along the 'Spittals' for 290 yards or thereabouts. The company intended to purchase land for this purpose and to obtain loans and mortgages as necessary. To fund the project, the company intended to levy tolls, rates and duties on vessels and boats using the harbour and impose an entrance fee for all persons wanting to enter the pier. Capital for the new company was raised by public subscription to a limited liability company raising £10,000 almost immediately. The total value of the share offer was to be £150,000.

The proposal initially attracted local support, and the following year, a meeting was held at Taylor's Hotel on The Crescent. Mr John Unett, who was in favour of the scheme and believed that 'the harbour' would be of great national benefit, chaired the meeting. Mr Unett concluded his address by formally presenting the committee with a purse containing 160 guineas. However, by April 1884, no harbour had been constructed and the shareholders were not able to raise the capital needed to take the project forward and in June 1884 the company was dissolved.

A less ambitious company named *Filey Fishery Harbour and Pier Co* was incorporated in May 1878, the chairman was Lord Claude John Hamilton. MP for Lynn and vice-president of The Great Northern Railway, other directors included Lord Londesborough and Christopher Sykes MP. However, once again this scheme never got off the ground.

During this time lack of government support was an issue. However, in January 1883, the government suggested that a harbour at Filey would be important for the defence of the country. The report suggested that the harbour could be built with the use of convict labour at a cost in the region of £1,250,000. The other consideration was a harbour at Dover, but Filey was the preferred location. However, Filey Brigg would have to have been expanded to create a new harbour entrance and would have become an imposing fort to house a prison extending towards Reighton Sands. The proposed prison would have been constructed and homed up to 750 inmates and provided cheap labour for the building of the scheme for up to twelve years.

Not surprisingly, the people of Filey were in an uproar and the preservation of the natural beauty of Filey was under threat. In the end, Langdon Prison was constructed on the white cliffs of Dover, although once more a lack of Government support prevailed, and Dover did not get its promised harbour until the turn of the 20th century. Filey would not be what it is today if its strong-minded people had not opposed this drastic plan to change to its landscape.

Langdon Prison, Dover (Credit Dover Museum)

Filey's Churches

St Oswald's Filey Parish Church

As discussed in a previous chapter, it is proposed that during the Middle Ages, and somewhere near the site of today's church, there stood an original ancient Saxon church dedicated to St Bartholomew. This was most likely in the field behind the present church. However, by the 16th century, this church was in ruins.

Tradition also points to the possibility of a village in this vicinity, as mounds were discovered some time back revealing buildings of different ages. These were possibly from the Beckwith and Buck families, but they could also be from an earlier period. Furthermore, in the mid-19th century, a stone thought to belong to the choir or part of the chancel of the old Norman church was dug up in a field west to the gate of the goods yard of the railway station. (now Tesco and Filey's workshops) For many years this stone was stored in the backyard of the T'Oard Ship Inn on Queen Street. In the same field, a few years previously an altar of approximately eighteen inches in length was dug up. No records remain of what happened to either of these artefacts.[3]

Artists impression of the chancel found near the Railway Station

3 W.S. Cortis *An Historical and Descriptive Guide to Filey.* (1861)

St Oswald's, Filey's parish church, is a magnificent ancient Grade 1 listed building, built under the reign of Stephen, and begun under the auspices of the Augustinian Canons at Bridlington, for whom a monastery had been founded by Filey's benefactor Walter de Gant. It is understood that initially, the Bridlington Canons will have supplied St Oswald's with the clergy. Eventually, a settlement of Canons settled in Filey, who selected one to be their head, whilst still being dependent on Bridlington.

The church has been described by the late renowned architectural historian Sir Nikolaus Pevsner as 'The finest church in the North-East corner of the East Riding's buildings of England. Many people have wondered why the church stands on its own away from the town. It does appear that it is isolated from the town itself. This takes us back to when there was a 'North & South 'Fieling'.'

The ravine separates the original village of Filey which stood on the north side under the rule of Pickering and Lythe in the North Riding. Whereas, years later, a village sprang up on the south side in the 'East Riding' where the market was held. Therefore, this part of the town grew it came under the wapentake of Dickering. According to Cole (1828) on the south side of the town was a place called *Chapel Island* upon which stood a *Chapel of Ease*. Unfortunately, no further information is recorded.

Nowadays it is easy to cross the bridge and visit the church, but in times gone by people went up and down the sides of the steep ravine by steps. There would have been a rapid stream of water flowing and only a small narrow bridge to cross it (Gentleman's Magazine, 1805). However, this bridge was destroyed by a great storm in 1857 and replaced by a sturdier iron bridge. So, going to church cannot have been an easy task. Interestingly, while the ravine marks the boundary between North and South, it gives credence to a local saying when referring to a person's final journey in that, 'He's gaing acrass ti' North.'

Filey Parish Church 1832

It is highly probable that stone used for the church's construction came from Filey's ancient quarry, which was located somewhere on the North Cliff. This was the same quarry that provided the stone for the building of Bridlington Priory on the orders of Walter de Gant. It is also likely that stone from the original late 12th century Saxon church was used, together with stone from early houses from the same area. Information also suggests that the stone from the original church could possibly have come from the Roman signal station that was in this area. Unfortunately, it is unlikely that this can be confirmed.

Filey, like many other churches in the country, adopted St Oswald as their patron saint. King Oswald was the first king to bring together church and state since Roman times, and he can be credited for uniting Britain and converting the English to Christianity. The tradition of state-backed religion started at Lindisfarne with the first monastery. This period is now referred to as 'The Golden Age of Lindisfarne' and was primarily responsible for some of the key moments in British history from the Crusades to the Reformation.

With the support of King Oswald, this monastery set up a school to teach reading and writing (in Latin). The monastery trained young boys as missionaries who spread the Gospel in England. Women were also encouraged to give themselves to God and become nuns. The Lindisfarne Gospels are prime examples of creative Christian skill, which survive today.

King Oswald was a popular king who ruled for eight years before he was defeated and dismembered in the battle of Maserfield between 641 and 642. Following his death, the brave pious king was canonised and venerated not only in England but all over Europe as a saint. King Oswald's legacy continued throughout the mediaeval period, as his bones and ashes were scattered around Europe and treasured by the religious communities which held them.

The writer, J.R.R Tolkien took inspiration from St Oswald (he was once a professor of Anglo-Saxon History at Oxford University) for his character of Aragorn in his novel 'The Hobbit'. Aragorn joins Frodo the Hobbit on a quest to destroy the King before returning to Gondor, the land of his ancestry, thus claiming his rightful place as king. Like the real King Oswald. It has also been suggested that King Oswald bears more than a striking resemblance to the hero in the Anglo-Saxons most cultural achievement and that he was the source of the inspiration behind the epic poem Beowulf.

The original design of the church was early gothic, and it had a nave only with a West Tower. There is space in the west wall for a staircase, and a window remains visible only from the outside. It is believed that the construction of this west tower was discontinued following the failure of the South West Pier. Early in the 20th century, a stone altar was found on the chancel floor where it had been placed in the 1500s probably during the reformation. A small cross can be seen on each of the four corners which are thought to represent where the nails pierced Christ's hands and feet when he was nailed to the cross, and a large one in the centre of the altar is thought to represent where the sword pierced His side. It could be that this altar possibly belonged to the old original Saxon church.

High in the tower are three musical bells, which bear the following inscriptions:

1st Bell

Fiat Voluntas Pater Omnipotence 1682

2nd Bell

Sole Deo Gloria Pax Hominibus 1700

3rd Bell

Gloria Deo In Excelsis 1675

(These inscriptions are transcribed from the original)

Through the centuries, the church has undergone many periods of restoration. It was restored in 1839, with contributions from Henry Bentley Esq (Ravine Villa) and several smaller subscribers. A valuable communion plate was donated by Joseph Stocks Esq and a new organ was presented to the church by Mrs Bentley of Ravine Hall.

It was partly rebuilt in 1885. At this time the plaster was removed from the walls revealing the original stonework for the first time in 700 years. Unfortunately, the walls were white-washed and many of the ancient features destroyed. A fire in 1908 almost destroyed the church completely. Fortunately, the alarm was called by a choir boy. The organ was destroyed, and this was replaced by the present organ which was built on the side of the chancel. However, the church needed a new roof. The spire was damaged by the Dogger-Bank Earthquake of 1932, which measured 6.1 on the Richter scale.

Methodists-Wesleyan & Primitive

In comparison to many other towns throughout the country, Methodism came relatively late to Filey. It is reported that the earliest meeting of the Wesleyan branch of the Methodist church was formed in 1811 at Back Lane (now Chapel Street). However, the chapel was not well attended with only 15 members. To recruit more people ministers preached through the streets, which did not go down well with Filey residents who often pelted the preachers with dried fish and anything else they had to hand. The ministers considered that Filey was a lost cause to include them in any branch of the Methodists society.

Filey people were stuck in their ways and were not easily won over; they were indifferent to change, especially when it came to religion. Prior to 1823, Filey was noted for being a village of 'vice and wickedness'. It was well known for its Sabbath-breaking, cock-fighting, gambling, swearing and whose people (both men and women) liked to get as drunk as they possibly could. The Methodist movement considered the town and its people 'lost causes'.

This all changed in 1823 when a Methodist minister named John Oxtoby or 'Praying Johnnie' as he was affectionately known came to town. He refused to give up on Filey. He was convinced that the people needed a vital religion to moralise them. John believed that the fishermen needed religion to give them the strength to cope with storms and imminent danger. The women too also needed religion to bear the strain of anxiety, and to comfort them in the times of desolation.

John Oxtoby was born in 1767, near Pocklington. For about fifteen years Oxtoby worked with the Wesleyan Methodists. He became an unofficial travelling itinerant working mainly as an exhorter and prayer leader. In 1819 he met William Clowes (one of the founders of Primitive Methodism) and became his right-hand man. John joined the Primitive Methodist Connexion, as he considered that many of the Primitive Methodists preachers were like-minded in their approach to mission.

The Wesleyan Methodists were formed by John Wesley. Wesley did not intend to find a new denomination, but historical circumstances and his organisational genius conspired against his desire to remain in the Church of England. Wesley's followers first met in private home 'societies.' When these societies became too large for members to care for one another, Wesley organised 'classes,' each with eleven members and a leader. Classes met weekly to pray, read the Bible, discuss their spiritual lives, and to collect money for charity. Men and women met separately, but anyone could become a class leader.

Moreover, John Wesley was convinced of the importance of education; thus, Wesleyan day schools were opened around the country. The Wesleyan favoured more ornate buildings and concentrated on the needs of more affluent and influential urban classes. Whereas the Primitive Methodists focused more on the role of laypeople and so concentrated on the rural poor.

In 1823, despite the misgivings of others, John refused to give up on Filey. The story goes that when walking up Muston Hill on his way to convince the people of Filey to change their ways, he caught sight of Filey and he fell to his knees and began to pray. He strongly believed that God would guide him. He rose from his knees shouting 'Filey is taken, Filey is taken!' From that day on there was a remarkable revival with lasting results, which laid the foundations of a strong cause in Filey. Originally, meetings were held in barns and sheds, however, demand was so strong that the Primitive Methodists built a chapel originally called Bethesda later to be known as The Albert Hall (now the Salvation Army).

Bethesda Chapel (The Albert Hall) Demolition 1974.

Credit Martin Douglas

The Wesleyan society shared in this religious revival, as did St Oswald's parish church. Therefore, the morals of the village were rapidly improved. Religion wrought for sobriety, thrift, better social manners, and domestic discord. It was the Filey fishermen who led the way in abandoning Sunday fishing. As it turned out, it was found that the men who fished for six days had a larger catch than those who worked for seven days.

By 1863, Filey had become a model fishing town. The Wesleyan Minister Rev. Edwin Day declared: 'This change was down to the Primitive Methodist Connexion.' Some prominent members helped to shape its popularity, namely, Mrs Gordon who was the wife of the coastguard. Mrs Gordon was well travelled and well educated and considered 'the queen of missionary collectors' who inspired others to do the same. A Mrs Jenkinson – known as 'Nan Jenk' – struck a deal with the fishermen whereby they would give to the missionary a percentage of all the fish they caught above a certain quota, on condition that Mrs Jenkinson would pray for them when they were fishing. Mrs Jenkinson's husband William also became converted and lived to see the 100th member of the society.

John Wyville (died 1866) was another of Filey's 'lost causes'. That is until John Oxtoby placed his hands on his shoulders and said: 'Thou must be converted, for the Lord has great work for you to do!' Not long after John joined the society, attended readings, cultivated his mind, and became an arduous and competent local preacher.

In 1865, simple but effective preaching was the success of Primitive Methodism, hence the chapel is known as 'Ranter' chapel. Filey fishermen became staunch followers of the Primitive Methodist connexion and they began to spread the word around Yorkshire and across the north. To get their message across they would spread the word of the Gospel in song, which was the beginning of The Filey fishermen's choir.

Primitive Methodism became such a popular Christian denomination in Filey that new premises were soon needed. Fundraising began, and legendary fish suppers were held to raise funds for a new chapel which would hold 900 people. A site was secured and in 1870 the foundation stone was laid in Union Street for a new chapel to be named 'Ebenezer'.

Ebenezer Chapel

FILEY CHAPEL.

Ebenezer 'Ranter' Chapel

Wesleyan Methodists, who had premises on the corner of Murray Street (later called The Victoria Rooms) and a day school (now Dixons Discount Warehouse) were also finding that their premises were inadequate. A new church with a 90-foot spire was built in the gothic style on the junction of Union Street and Station Avenue. It was designed by Mr Petch of Scarborough at a cost of £4,700 and erected using local tradesman. The church, originally called Trinity Methodist Church, opened in 1876. It accommodated 600 people on the ground floor and 100 children in the lobby gallery. There was also a large schoolroom with four classrooms above it. A mysterious fire destroyed most of this building in 1918 and the church was rebuilt; it reopened its doors in 1923.

In the early 1970s, it was becoming apparent that it would be advantageous to merge the two Methodist congregations, and Ebenezer closed its doors for the last time in May 1975, after 104 years of service. The two congregations were from that day known as Filey Methodists and continue to this day.

Filey Methodist Church

St Mary's Church and The Sisters of Charity of Our Lady of Evron

Perrine Thulard (1654-1735) was born in Chapelle au Riboul in Mayenne, France on the 6th November 1654. At the age of twenty-five, she became a widow and decided to dedicate her life to God and dedicate her time to the teaching of young girls, the care of the sick and the welfare of those less fortunate. Hence, Perrine's work became well known and other young girls became associated with her project, and together they formed 'The Society of Daughters of Charity.'

Following the French Third Republic anti-clerical legislation it became difficult for religious orders to continue teaching in France, subsequently, the sisters decided to extend their order to England. The sisters established their first congregation in Filey in 1904. Prior to this Roman Catholics did not have a presence in the town. Thus, Father Eugene Roulin, a French Benedictine Monk was appointed by Ampleforth Abbey to act as chaplain to the sisters and he became the town's first resident Roman Catholic Priest. Father Roulin was a very charismatic character and oversaw the architecture and design of the building of St Mary's Catholic Church in Brooklands. Father Roulin and the nuns were a welcome and much-respected sight in Filey, their presence brought an increase in Catholic visitors to the town and a welcome boost for local businesses.

The nuns purchased the property at 1 & 2 South Crescent Villas which were enlarged, and the convent school opened on the Feast of the Sacred Heart in 1909. In addition to the boarding school, the sisters also ran a parish school known as 'The Villa School' so-called because the school was at the foot of the cliffs at the Villa Ambrosia (now 21, The Beach). This 'Free' school was devoted to the less well-off children in Filey and fulfilled the initial mission of the sisters of Evron.

In 1913, the convent advertised adult education classes for anyone over the age of twelve. The sisters offered classes in 'cutting out, sewing and mending, every weekday evening at a cost of threepence per session. Fancy needlework cost an additional three pence.

Despite the First World War, the school continued to expand, and by 1921 there were 102 pupils, 22 of which were full-time boarders increasing to 70 boarders by 1950. While most pupils were girls, the school did teach boys up to the age of eight, including Charles Laughton who went on to be a famous actor and Hollywood film star. The convent-educated other famous people including Lana Bowen-Woods who, under the pen name Sara Woods, became a very successful crime writer. Like most schools of this era the regime was strict, but the education thorough and long-lasting.

Over the next thirty years, the increase in pupils necessitated expansion including a large dormitory for younger boarders, gymnasium, and cloakrooms. An average school day started at 7.30 with breakfast, then Mass in the Convent Chapel then perhaps a game of hockey on the beach or the curriculum lessons including French taught by the native speaking nuns. Homework was followed by a supper of bread and cocoa, prayers and bed.

The school uniform was easily recognisable, and the girls were a familiar sight around Filey in the winter dressed in their black felt or velour hats, navy blue coats and dresses. The summer costume was navy blue, a white dress, gloves and a Panama hat. The dormitories slept four to a room with each girl having their own chair and bedside table. Initially, the convent had no running water, and no heating except for oil stoves. Eventually, the school installed bathrooms, which the borders shared.

Father Eugene Roulin died 31st March 1939 aged seventy-eight in a Leeds Nursing Home. A few years earlier, he had an accident in which he broke his leg. His age and failing health did not allow the broken bone to repair itself, and this was a big disappointment to the active father, who subsequently resigned himself to his faith and religion. Filey is proud of the heritage he has left behind.

Sadly, following the arrival of the comprehensive education system in the late 1960s, the convent school closed, as Filey had no other comparable school with which to merge. The nuns left Filey for their various apostolates elsewhere and the building, purchased by Scarborough Urban District Council, which became Filey's Town Hall. Today the building is the Evron Centre and a plaque denotes a mark of respect for the nuns who selflessly made a lasting impact on its pupils and the people of Filey. The Evron centre now serves as both a Community and Business centre, with meeting rooms, a lecture room, and Concert Hall.

A Filey Convent School 'Old Girl' reunion get together happens each year on the first weekend after Easter.

St John the Evangelist and the Iron Church

St John's credit Margaret Rounding

In the mid-19th century, there was a revival of religion and gospel studies from all religious denominations. The Industrial Revolution had gripped the country and with the implantation of the railways, people began to move around the country more freely. This was especially apparent in the seaside towns throughout the summer months when demand for church services increased. Throughout the country, new churches were built, and old ones renovated and modernised. Filey was no exception, especially in the summer season when St Oswald's Church was full. Furthermore, many of Filey's visitors were staying at the other side of town making access to the parish church more difficult. Therefore, it was deemed necessary for a new Anglican church to be built in the town.

Tin-tabernacles or Galvanised Corrugated Iron Churches were an ideal solution to Filey's problem. This type of church could be constructed quickly and would provide a temporary solution whilst funds were raised to build a more permanent church building. In 1857 land for such a church was found at the east side of West Avenue midway between Brooklands and Southdene. However, the purchase of this structure was the subject of a London Court case. It seems that the decision to purchase this church was made by Miss Catherine Legard who is described in the court documents as 'A Lady of Fortune' and a relative of the Legard family of Ganton, who at that time owned North Cliff Villa in Filey. By all accounts, Miss Legard had seen the structure in a catalogue whilst visiting an exhibition at the Crystal Palace London. She had agreed with the manufacturer Mr Hemming of Bow to purchase the Iron Church at a cost of £750 which would be erected and delivered solely on Miss Legard's credit.

Iron Church era 1857 – West Avenue-Credit-Filey Town Council

However, it seems that other members of the congregation were not impressed with the idea of such a structure for their church and preferred to wait for a more permanent one. The Rev. Thomas Norfolk Jackson is reported to say, 'Having foolishly (assumed) all risks of an Iron church, we are in an anomalous state.'

Subsequently, when the church was nearly completed and ready to be sent by railway to Filey, there were significant differences of opinion regarding the design and structure of the church. Hence, the church was not erected, and Mr Hemming found himself considerably out of pocket and sued Miss Legard in the London Courts for breach of contract and damages.

The hearing was held in February 1857, at the Court of Common Pleas in London in front of a special jury. After hearing evidence for the plaintiff, his Lordship suggested that Miss Legard asked the plaintiff to erect a church and that is what he had done and that by not accepting the church Miss Legard was in breach of contract. The jury agreed and found in favour of the plaintiff. Miss Legard accepted responsibility and the Iron Church was erected as a temporary measure in Filey. The incumbent was Reverend Thomas Norfolk Jackson who delivered a daily service at half-past ten and three o'clock each day.

In 1864, Admiral Robert Mitford of Hunmanby Hall was a patron of the parish. He donated a piece of land on West Avenue on which to build a new church. The curate Rev. Pettit and his friends raised a sum of £1,500 towards the cost of the new church of St John the Evangelist and the balance of £700 was raised by parishioners. The church built in a geometric architectural style, consisting of a nave and chancel with transepts. There is a stained-glass window on the east side, which is dedicated to the memory of Admiral Mitford.

The church was consecrated in 1870 and licensed in 1874. The church was altered again in the 1970s when the building was converted to provide a smaller church and a much-needed church hall.

Filey's Interesting Incumbents

The Reverend Evan Williams

Filey's parish church of St Oswald's has had many incumbents, but in the early 19th century, two are particularly remembered for their eccentricities. The first one could explain the growing disillusionment with the institutionalist status quo of religion in the town.

Between the years 1809 and 1833 The Rev. Evan Williams was a curate (St Oswald's). At that time, there was no vicarage, so he lived alone at 33 Church Street. He would never enter by the door and always went in and out of the house by the windows. Further peculiarities of his were that he would never let any women in the house and that when the local dairyman delivered milk to the property he had to do it via a pitcher that the Reverend would let down on a rope from an upstairs window. He would only spend one shilling's worth of fish for his food each week. Also, at church, he would begin a service then say there was no sermon and would go home locking the church door behind him. It is hoped that he let the congregation out first.

An interesting story is told about him in 1823 when at the bedside of one of the parishioners who lay dying, the unfortunate man asked that he may receive the last sacrament and it is recorded that the conversation went as follows:

Rev. 'Do you swear?'

Sick man 'No.'

Rev. 'Do you ever get drunk?'

Sick man 'No.'

Rev. 'Do you owe any money?'

Sick man 'No.'

Rev. 'Well you are alright then! But you do owe me money for your father's gravestone. I cannot give you the sacrament until you have paid it!'

The dying man settled the bill with the Reverend and received absolution and died satisfied.

Rev. Williams was not happy with the way churchwardens were selected, whereby instead of them being the choice of one by the parishioners and one by the vicar at St Oswald's, it had always been customary for both to be selected by the parishioners. Reverend Williams challenged this tradition in court, but his lawsuit found favour with the established tradition, at a cost of £90 to the church.

The Reverend Arthur Neville Cooper

Credit Stephen Eblet

Later in the 19th century, the Reverend Arthur Neville Cooper became the vicar of Filey. In 1905, he told his parishioners that he was the only incumbent in England who was not allowed to nominate a churchwarden. This right had been withdrawn from the vicar of Filey some years earlier when the churchwardens sold the lead from the church roof to buy food for starving parishioners.

Reverend Cooper earned the title 'The Walking Parson', as in 1886 he walked from London to Filey, (200 miles.) A year later he walked to Rome, some 743 miles. In the succeeding year, he walked repeatedly across Ireland. Then from Hamburg to Paris. He also walked extensively across Belgium, Spain and through Venice. The Reverend Cooper walked at a pace of 30 miles per day, but on one occasion between breakfast and supper, he covered 48 miles. When asked how he did this he said the reason was that he carried no luggage, except what he could fit into a rucksack which he carried on his back. He even tore up letters he received on his journey to ensure he did not have any excess weight. The Rev. Cooper acquired his passion for walking while working as a clerk in London, where he was obliged to walk through all weathers four miles every morning, repeating the same journey on his journey home.

Before setting off on his journey, Reverend Cooper would study the language of the country he was travelling to. He thought this to be essential as some of the towns he visited were small and he wanted to converse with the locals.

S.14852. REV CANON A. N. COOPER VICAR OF FILEY.
(THE WALKING PARSON)

The Local Workhouse

Low Hall Hunmanby

Low Hall, on Sands Lane, Hunmanby became the workhouse for the area in 1785. This workhouse had an average of 16 inmates and took in paupers from around the parish including Filey, Flamborough, Burton Fleming, and many others.

The cost to convert the workhouse was an expensive undertaking, costing £200 to make it fit for purpose, £87.5s was collected from the poor rates, £26.4s was borrowed from Squire Osbaldeston (Hunmanby Hall), and £60 was given to the house from the 'town stock'. Equipment purchased included sheets, baking dishes, coal, and food. Although the food at the workhouse was ample, it lacked variety and vitamin content. It appears that although meat, potatoes and molasses were on the menu, there is no mention of any green vegetables on any surviving workhouse diet sheets.

The workhouse was hated by the poor, and the government were terrified of encouraging lazy people, so they made sure that people feared it, and families knew that it was the 'last resort' and would do anything to keep out of it. The reason for ending up in the workhouse varied, usually because people were too poor, old, or ill to support themselves, lack of work, high unemployment, or no family willing to support them through poverty or illness. Unmarried pregnant women were often disowned by their families, and the workhouse became their only option. Interestingly, the master of the poor house in 1791 was a Mr Thomas Dinnis, who himself fell down on his luck when he was discharged from his duty and paid off. He went to Scarborough races in August of that year and lost all his money on a horse. He was subsequently declared destitute and faced bankruptcy proceedings at York Assizes.

Here is a very brief history of what happened to 'poor households' prior to the abolition of the Poor Act in 1929 when the Poor Unions were abolished, and the administration of poor relief was transferred to the counties and their boroughs.

From 1601, The Poor Law Act allowed local parishes to look after their poor. These poor people could live at home and claim assistance from the wealthier householders of the local parishes. As is much the same today, these upper and middle-class people were not impressed, and they assumed that their money was being spent on lazy people, who were simply avoiding work, especially as the cost of providing for these people was growing more expensive year by year. A fairer system was sought, to avoid the current system being abused by scroungers and the like; and after years of upper-class complaints, the Poor Law was introduced in 1834.

When this new Poor Law was introduced many of the old parishes formed poor law unions, who essentially clubbed together to provide a workhouse for their community. Following the introduction of this act, poor people, who previously would have relied on a parish handout to survive and provide for their families, were no longer allowed to live at home. Instead, they were expected to work hard, and if not they and their families were sent to live in the workhouse.

Over the years, there have been various legacies left to the poor. One of the earliest recorded was in August 1697 when a yeoman named Elisha Trott from Muston, left an annuity to the poor of Filey in the amount of 20 shillings, which was payable out of a house and land he owned in Cayton named *The Rooks*. The will did stipulate that 'If the tenant of the said property withholds the payment, the overseers or churchwardens shall enter the house and remain until it is paid.'

This law did not account for tramps and vagrants, who were a police matter. Subsequently, tramps and vagrants were known as 'the houseless poor', and if caught would have to be set in the stocks for three days and three nights. They were fed only on bread and water. If one of these vagabonds were to be found begging, then it would be customary for them to be stripped naked from the waist upwards and whipped until their bodies bled. A tramp or vagrant could be someone who was a shipwrecked seaman, a fortune teller, an Egyptian or a gipsy, or even a discharged prisoner. The worst type of vagrant, who was considered the scum of the earth, was an able-bodied person refusing to work for the current rate of pay.

Hunmanby Workhouse closed in 1836 when Hunmanby joined the Bridlington Union and a large purpose-built workhouse for 150 inmates built in Marton Road Bridlington. After 1930, the poor law system ended, and Bridlington workhouse was taken over by East Riding County Council, and renamed Burlington House, to provide accommodation for geriatric patients.

The Atlee Labour Government of 1945-1950, introduced the welfare state and the workhouse system was finally abolished.

Old Filey

Ever since the Norman Conquest, the manorial rights of Filey seem to have appertained to the Lords of Hunmanby. Gilbert de Gant was succeeded by his son, Walter de Gant, who founded Bridlington Priory. At this time, Filey Church had no incumbent but was served by a stipendiary priest provided by Bridlington Priory. Six of the Gants in succession have held this Manor, some of whom appear to have given lands in Ganton to Bridlington Priory. Most probably, the village of Ganton derives its name from this prominent family.

The Gant's were succeeded by Ralph de Neville, who gave half a carucate of land to the same priory. His son also named Ralph gave 'to God, and to the church and monks of Bridlington, the stone and stone quarry of Filey for building their monastery, and all their offices.'

Filey was evidently a fishing town of some note, as the Abbots of Bridlington, Whitby and Grimsby quarrelled about the tithes. In 1122, the first prior had a dispute with the Abbot of Whitby, which was arranged by arbitration of the Dean and Chapter of York that when Filey fishermen put into Whitby, they should there pay tithes, and when the fishermen of Whitby put into Filey they should pay tithes at Filey. However, further disputes arose, for in 1190, Hugh, Abbot of Bridlington, complained to the Court of Rome of injustice done to him: when the pope, Celestine, commissioned the Abbot of Rievaulx and the Priors of Kirkham and Warter to examine the case. These arbiters decided that the Abbot of Whitby should never more molest the fishermen of Filey when they went into that port and obliged him to relinquish all claim to any tithe from them.

Changing Street Names and Demolished 'Yards and Rents'

The earliest detailed map of Filey dates to 1788 and is 'The Enclosure Map.' At this time Filey basically consisted of two streets – Town Street (now Queen Street) and Church Street at right angles to it. The frontage of these streets was densely built up around both sides of Town Street and to the west of Church Street, which both had elongated 'yards' or tenements running on the south side of Town Street and the west side of Church Street to 'Back Lanes' which are now Mitford Street and Scarborough Road.

This arrangement is typical of English settlements in the 12th century onwards and prior to 1788 the structure of a main street and back lanes was little changed since medieval times. Following 'Enclosure' many of Filey's street names changed, with some streets or 'rents or yards' (as they were known) disappeared completely.

A substantial selection of land in Filey was advertised for sale in the Yorkshire Gazette in 1855, including 'Back Lane' which then became Mitford Street with new houses and shops.

AT FILEY,
In the East Riding of the County of York.

TO BE SOLD BY AUCTION, at the PACK-HORSE INN, in FILEY, in the East-Riding of the County of York, on FRIDAY, the 9th day of November next at TWO o'Clock in the Afternoon, (subject to such conditions as shall then be read,) Mr. ROBT ALLISON, Auctioneer, the whole of the Valuable PROPERTY, as follows, viz. :—

LOT 1.—All that Freehold DWELLING-HOUSE, situate in the Front Street in Filey aforesaid, with a Yard and Garden behind the same, now in the occupation of Mary Bulmer.

LOT 2.—A Freehold DWELLING-HOUSE, adjoining to the last-named Cottage on the East, with a Yard and Garden behind the same, now in the occupation of Grace Robinson.

LOT 3.—Three Freehold DWELLING-HOUSES, two of them in the Front Street, and one of them in the Back Lane, with a Yard behind, now in the occupation of William Cammish, Thomas Holmes, and John Cowling.

LOT 4.—A Freehold DWELLING-HOUSE, in the Back Lane, with a Yard behind, now in the occupation of John Chapman.

LOT 5.—A Freehold DWELLING-HOUSE and SHOP, in the Back Lane, with a Yard behind the same, now in the occupation of William Marshall.

LOT 6.—A Piece of Freehold GROUND adjoining the last-mentioned lot on the South, with several small Erections thereon, containing 198 square yards or thereabouts, now in the occupation of Messrs. Cammish, Cowling, Marshall, and Chapman.

LOT 7.—A Piece of Freehold LAND, principally used as a Garden, adjoining Lot 6 on the South, containing 284 square yards or thereabouts, at present in the occupation of William Marshall and John Chapman.

LOT 8.—Two DWELLING-HOUSES, in the Front Street, and Two behind, with a large Piece of GROUND behind the Dwelling-Houses, containing 1,444 square yards or thereabouts, at present in the occupation of Francis Clifford, Robert Wiseman, William Sayer, and Benjamin Grice. A Communication to this Lot from the Back Street will be reserved.

LOT 9.—A Piece of Freehold GROUND, admirably adapted for a Building Site, containing 669 square yards or thereabouts, situate behind the Pack-Horse Inn, and fronting the Back Street on the South, at present in the occupation of Mary Storey.

LOT 10.—A Piece of Freehold GROUND, adjoining the last-mentioned Lot on the East, containing 859 square yards, having the same frontage, and being similarly adapted to building purposes as Lot 9, also in the occupation of Mary Storey.

For further Particulars apply to the Auctioneer, at Bridlington; to Mr. Sheriton, Hunmanby, where a plan of the premises may be seen; or to

Messrs. BRUMELL,
Solicitors, Morpeth.

Yards

Off Murray Street, in between what is now Filey Bistro and The Three Tuns was Cambridge Yard. In 1905, a Captain Robert Groves who was the Head of Filey's Fire Brigade is recorded as living at no 8. All the houses are now demolished. On the same street, there were also five houses in what was Jennings Yard (where Smart's Stores are now).

There were many 'yards' off Queen Street, such as White's Yard between houses 61-63. Then Richardson's Yard situated between 75 and 77 Queen Street which consisted of five houses all of them occupied by fishermen and their families. Stockdale yard was in between 81 Queen Street, and what was Goodlad's Grocers (1905) again all the houses have since been demolished. Stockdale Yard housed fishermen with surnames we still see today, such as Sayers, Jenkinson, Cammish, Scotter, Watkinson and Cowling. It is also reported that a monkey was kept in a cage in one of the fishermen's back-yards.

At 41 Church Street stands Wenlock House which was named after Lady Wenlock who was a regular visitor and admirer of Filey. This house is marked by an anchor that was found in Filey Bay. In 1892 this was the home of the Suggitt family who owned the coble Zillah named after Mrs Suggitt. This is the same family whose son Thomas met his demise in tragic circumstances after plunging to his death on Filey Brigg whilst looking for natural artefacts.

Between Wenlock House and number 39, and through a narrow passage stood 9 houses known as Wenlock Place. The 1851 census records 60 people lived there. Private George William Skelton was born at no 5 Wenlock Place in 1893. He joined the Coldstream Guards and fought in the Great War but lost his life aged 23 and died from gunshot wounds to the chest and abdomen.

Changing Street Names

41-51 Mitford Street, previously Alma Terrace

Chapel Street, previously Brick Garth

27-41 West Avenue, previously Clarence Terrace

3-21 Scarborough Road – East Parade

Between 7-8 The Crescent, previously Middle Street

Belle Vue Street, previously North Street

42-46 Belle Vue Street, previously Prospect Place

89-103 West Avenue, previously Ravine Bank

Crescent Hill, previously Ravine Road

24-38 Rutland Street, previously Rutland Terrace

Reynolds Street, previously Skelton Lane

Between 14-15 The Crescent, previously South Street Station Road, previously Summerville Road.

10-14 Station Road, previously Moore Lane & West End Terrace

38-54 West Avenue, previously Westfield Terrace

West Road, originally Common Right Road

Filey's Ancient Market and Fair

On the site of where now stands the Forge Garage once stood Filey's courthouse. This area was aptly named Court-Garth and is said to have been the Court of Bridlington Prior for the dispensing of justice and the transaction of business. In later years, around this area was the house of Filey vicarage which is now Ebenezer Terrace.

The vicinity of the Court House was also the place of Filey's ancient market, which was initially held on a Sunday. However, on 22nd August 1240, King Henry 111 made a grant to William de Neville that the day of the market would in future be changed to Friday. The reason given was that this market was damaging Gilbert de Gant's market at Hunmanby. However, this was not the end of this disagreement, as in the autumn of 1242, Gilbert de Gant brought a case against William de Neville, regarding the market at Filey, contending that William had broken this final concord. On 29th May 1256, King Henry 111 granted the burgesses of Scarborough, the right to plead in the king's name in his court for the abolition of Filey market and its fair, and that the markets of Sherbourne, and Brompton, were also suppressed for the benefit of Scarborough, which was rapidly increasing in size.

The market cross was located at the junction of Church Street and Scarborough Road, Mitford Street and Station Road (originally Moore Lane) and West Road (originally Common Right Lane) leading to Corn Mill, where the streets were widened out to form a small market place most likely dating from 1221.

Queen Street. The Hub of the Community

Queen Street was the centre of the community and for many years housed the families of most of the village. Morning greetings from the street's many fishermen as they made their way to their boats would be a common thing. Fishing was an integral part of the town, and many of the fishermen's houses were defined by a glazed coble or drifter in their front door panel. Unfortunately, many of these have disappeared or replaced.

Over the years, Queen Street has been known by a few different names. In the late 18th century it was named Town Street as it was the main street in the town. Following this, from Cliff Top to Reynolds Street it was Queen Street and the rest was King Street. The street was buzzing with shops and craftsmen including fishermen and rope makers.

In the mid-19th century, the residents in the newly established 'New Filey' were often born from outside the town and did not have the same sense of closeness, or community that the 'old Filey' residents had. King/Queen Street was a major thoroughfare with lots of shops supplying most of the needs of the community, and there was no need for anyone to venture elsewhere not even to 'New Filey'. The only people that had to cross Murray Street on a regular basis were the girls and women who were working in the new hotels and boarding houses on the 'other' side of town.

Numbers 8-10 Queens street is now the museum but was previously a farm cottage and a fisherman's cottage. The post office was originally at number 79 then later moved to the corner of King Street and Reynolds Street before moving to Murray Street.

In 1895, Filey formed its own Urban District Council, in purpose-built offices at 52 King/Queen Street. Its first elected chairman was Mr W Maley. In addition, they formed a Highway, Improvement, Finance, and Fire Brigade Committee. A resolution adopted to the effect that £1,900 be borrowed at an interest rate of 3.5% to be repaid over 30 years from the Wolverhampton Corporation Sinking Food and Stock to meet the cost of drainage for the new offices. The council advertised in the local press for a clerk of works to oversee the laying out of the foreshore. Subsequently, a Mr William Gofton and his grandfather were appointed at a salary of forty-five pounds per year. However, works on the seashore were not satisfactory and the Council refused to pay the contractors, which ended up in litigation proceedings in the High Court.

Health was a major consideration in the town and Filey Urban District Council appointed a medical officer, Mr T Haworth, who presented his first report in January 1896. His findings for the quarter ending 31st December 1895 stated that there had been 22 births, and 12 deaths, seven of which were over the age of sixty, two between the ages of 50-60 and two infants under the age of two, and one premature birth. Deaths for the whole year totalled 76, which was higher than the national average, but Mr Haworth said that 27 of the deaths were children under twelve months and 23 over the age of sixty and that problems of pneumonia, influenza and bronchitis had attributed to the deaths in the very young and the very old. Mr Haworth also reported that the town was free from infectious diseases, remarking that the new drainage system had improved the sanitary conditions of the town, which now competed favourably with all other seaside resorts.

Many of the public houses on Queen/King Street remain such as The Foords, and The Grapes but a few of them have gone. The Pack Horse at 78 Queen Street was a thatched property, whose last licensee was a lady called Elizabeth Kilby before the premises were demolished and The Crown Hotel erected in its place. The Britannia stood on the corner which is now 65-71 Queen Street and whose last landlord was a Mr Edward Gutherless, who in 1882 was charged with keeping his house open beyond permitted hours, the coastguard John Hilman and a labourer William Crow were also charged with 'drinking after time'. However, following a court appearance, all charges were dropped when it was confirmed that both men were friends of the landlord, and no money had changed hands for the drinks. Not long after the premises were deemed to be unfit for purpose, and demolished.

Queen Street still retains an affectionate remembrance for many people, although sadly long gone are the various shops, pubs, fishermen's cottages, rents and yards, however, there remains an ambience for many people to recall the atmosphere of this once bustling, vigorous street that to this day makes it such a vital part of the community.

Filey Builds a New Sea Wall

Old Sea Wall

Prior to the building of the sea wall in 1894, Filey's foreshore was divided into two parts. One part was protected by a wooden hulking, the second part supported by damaged and corroding cliffs. These cliffs had taken a pounding from years from ferocious storms and powerful seas. A particularly severe storm in 1864 dislodged hundreds of tonnes of earth, washing away not only part of the cliffs, but also had a dramatic effect on the staple trade of the town. The fishing community was concerned that should there be another storm the fishermen would not be able to go to and from their landing, which at the time was their only available access to their cobles and their livelihoods.

Coble Landing Prior to the new Sea Wall

Coastal erosion continues to be a serious problem, and the need for a new sea-wall was considered as early as 1874, as the sea was making serious inroads into the cliffs, which unquestionably became a dominant consideration, as the land was disappearing at the rate of two yards a year, and unless something was done the houses on the foreshore would be swept away. Furthermore, plans for a harbour scheme had not come to fruition. Therefore, an ambitious plan was put in place to protect the foreshore and provide Filey with a most fashionable promenade.

Work on a new sea wall for the town started in 1892 when a committee was formed consisting of forty Filey residents (all men). The president was Mr Edwin Martin, (Martin's Ravine, Martin's Barrier) who kindly donated £100 towards the expenses for the opening ceremony. His stipulation to this generous offer was that the poor of the town were not hassled for donations towards the scheme.

The building of the wall was not without its problems, many of the town's ratepayers objected to the cost of the project, and there were many other obstacles to overcome. Consent from the Admiralty was required, and they had also to agree to waive their rights to the foreshore. Interestingly, had the Filey local board not proposed the plan when they did, then it would have been the Admiralty's responsibility to step in and protect the coastguard cottages.

The owners of the properties fronting the foreshore had to agree to either contribute to the cost of the scheme or grant concessions over their property. Difficulties had arisen when gaining consent from Miss Elizabeth Elders of Church Cliff farm, one of Filey's biggest landowners with over 272 acres. Eventually, this was overcome, and a provisional order obtained giving the committee the go-ahead.

The board advertised for competent plans to be drawn. Engineers Messrs Fairbank & Sons, Driffield & Westminster were appointed, with James Dickson of St. Albans contracting the building work. The cost to build the sea wall was estimated to be £12,000 and a loan for this amount was arranged from the Ecclesiastical Commissionaires, one of the stipulations being that the loan must be repaid in full within ten years. (Due to unforeseen circumstances, the cost of the wall escalated to £15,000.) The Admiralty contributed £300 towards the scheme.

After discussion with the committee, Lord of the Manor, Colonel Mitford, Hunmanby Hall made stone available from the Brigg at a cost of one farthing per tonne. In October 1893 work began, and 2,000 tonnes of cement were delivered across the beach to form a railway from the Brigg to allow 20,000 tonnes of stone and shingle to be easily transported.

The length of the sea wall from Ravine Slipway to Crescent Hill is 700 yards. The plans considered the depressed road surface in front of the Spa saloon, which back then was continually flooded in high water and eroding rapidly. A slipway was built parallel to the wall. A margin of grass of about ten yards was constructed, with seats, and alcoves which were not only aesthetic but also provided rest for the weary traveller.

In front of a large lively crowd, the first of 20,000 concrete blocks were laid in April 1893 by Mrs Martin of Ravine Hall. The contractor's son Mr James Dickson handed Mrs Martin a silver trowel and ivory mallet which was inscribed: 'Presented to Mrs Edwin Martin, on her laying the first block of the Filey sea wall and promenade, 24th April 1893. Engineers Fairbank & Co; contractor James Dixon.'

Then to a proud and excited crowd, Mrs Martin gave three taps of the mallet and the block was laid into place, and she declared in a distinct voice, 'I declare this block properly laid.' Reverend A.N. Cooper blessed the wall and those engaged in the building of it.

Laying the foundation stone

The trowel and mallet used by Mrs Martin remain in the possession of Filey Town Council. Over two hundred men were employed in the construction who besides having their own missionary, were also provided with evening classes on reading and writing by local school teachers Miss Pym and Miss Brown.

The contractors completed the building works on schedule. The wall opened in June 1894, to a rejoicing town in party mode, and with their characteristic Yorkshire hospitality the townsfolk had decorated the town with coloured streamers and welcomed visitors from all over the country with signs saying: 'Welcome to Filey'.

The opening ceremony was conducted by Lord Herries, the Lord-Lieutenant of the East Riding. Lord Herries was presented with an ornamental key, the wards of which formed an 'H' and bore suitable inscriptions, the key being surmounted with a coronet. Lord Herries then unlocked a temporary wooden barrier and declared the sea wall open to the public, followed by tremendous applause.

It must be noted, that without the determination and providence of this committee of people who despite many obstacles and objections persevered and provided the town with not only a necessary defence barrier but their fortuitous foresight with regards the design of the promenade added a new era to the town's popularity as a holiday resort. Securing Filey's position as the jewel of the Yorkshire coast for many years to come.

THE NEW SEA-WALL AT FILEY, FORMALLY OPENED BY LORD HERRIES ON TUESDAY

Lord Herries opens the Sea Wall

The Fishing Industry

An early picture of the Coble Landing

For centuries, the staple trade of Filey has predominately been fishing. Sadly, in October 2013, this all changed when the last coble *Kathryn and Sarah* owned by Julian Barker left Filey, thus ending centuries of family tradition, hard work and industry. This coble was taken to Bridlington, refurbished and renamed *The Helena*. This is a far cry from 1858 when Filey fishery was at its maximum strength when most of the town's inhabitants had some connection with fishing in their families.

Prior, to the Industrial Revolution, Fishing and the sale of wool were the source of the nation's wealth and sustenance. As early as AD 211 there was a great abundance of fish along the northern shores of

Britain; Dion Cassius and Solinus, the latter of whom stated that the people of The Hebrides derived a principal part of their food from fishing, remarked on this and in 836 we note that the Netherlanders visited the North-East coast for the purposes of buying salt-fish.

By the late 1500s, it was reported that the Dutch fishing industry was very strong; so much so that in 1603 Sir Walter Raleigh laid before the King a pamphlet urging the advantages of vigorous prosecution. His reasoning is that the greatest amount of fish ever known in the world was on the Yorkshire Coast, yet the English people derived no benefit from it. They exported no herrings, yet the 'low' countries and other smaller states fished herring mainly along these coasts with an annual income of £1,700. Prior to this, it was the custom of Hollanders and Flemings before they began to fish on the Yorkshire Coast to 'crave leave' (seek permission) from the Governor of Scarborough Castle. In 1608 they paid a tribute to King James for this privilege, and in 1635 they paid to King Charles no less than £30,000 for permission to fish in the English seas. A colossal amount of money in those days.

As previously mentioned, 1857 was a successful year for Filey's fishermen, with a reported fleet of 64 inshore cobles, 17 herring cobles and 34 yawls. The coble was the most common, with numbers of them spotted not only on coble landing but all over the town, in gardens and in yards. Fishing follows a year-round pattern, whereby the yawls which were laid out in Scarborough over winter, would be refitted out ready for the season which begins in February to early June to line-fish for cod, halibut, and haddock. Each Yawl was manned by 6 men and 3 boys. They carried two coble's and mainly fished off the Dogger Bank. Mid-week the fish caught would be collected and put onto one Yawl which would then take it to market at Hull, Scarborough or Filey, leaving a coble and three men to continue fishing the remainder of the week. The gross proceeds were divided into seven shares. One belonging to the boat, out of which expenses paid, and the rest then paid between the remaining men who provided the lines, bait etc.

The coble was mostly used in winter and was manned by three men who each took with them 3 lines – 700 yards long and carrying 140 hooks. They each travelled as far as six miles out to sea in winter between December and January. Filey fishermen took on the dangerous waves while the larger boats lay by. At daybreak, Filey cobles went out to fish not knowing when or if they would return. Twenty stones of fish at that time was a good average catch for each coble, consisting of haddock, codlings, and 'spring fish' (between a codling and a cod). The year 1857 was a very successful one, with overall takings of £27,000 (a substantial amount, £2134,620.00 in today's currency – 2016.)

The Fishing trade is hazardous and is weather-dependent, with the town benefitting greatly from a 'Good Fishing Season' with most of the proceeds distributed around the town in wages, purchases and tradesmen. Other areas benefitted from this success such as the net manufacturers of Scotland, the rope and sailmakers of Hull, and the shareholders of The North-Eastern Railway, who benefited from the two thousand pounds a year cost to import herring around the country.

Filey Fishermen with their nets

Bonzo Filey's Pet Seal

While fishing on Filey Brigg in January 1927 local man Jack 'Bonzo' Jenkinson found a baby seal. The pub was in bad condition and weighed only one stone. Mr Jenkinson rescued it named it Bonzo and in time the seal would perform tricks. Bonzo was housed in a tank initially in Providence Place (Jenk Alley) then on Coble Landing. The tank required a change of fresh-water daily. Bonzo lived on a diet of fresh fish and was a constant attraction and source of amusement to visitors including the Princes Royal's two sons when they holidayed in Filey.

Mr Jenkinson charged visitors a 'copper' to watch Bonzo do tricks and push his snout in and out of the water.

Twelve years later Bonzo weight twenty stone and needed more and more water. In 1939, Mr Jenkinson's brother was looking after Bonzo when a bailiff from Filey Town Council called on him on a bicycle. The bailiff had court papers stating that Mr Jenkinson owed £20 in unpaid water-charges and demanded that 'he had come to take Bonzo.' Bearing in mind the size of the seal it doesn't seem that the bailiff had thought the logistics of how he was going to remove the seal especially as the only transport the bailiff had was a bike.

Mr Jenkinson was devastated, and news of the seal's fate soon spread around the country, offers flooded in one from Golden Acre Park Leeds who were willing to take the seal. Mr Jenkinson was adamant that the seal should stay in Filey and hoped that he could come to an arrangement with the council. However, it transpired that Mr Jenkinson had also not been able to afford the rent on the shed which housed Bonzo, thus Mr Jenkinson was given twenty-eight days to vacate and find another house for the seal. Filey Town council were unrepentant and obtained an order from the court to allow them to put the seal up for auction. At the last minute, an agreement was reached when Mr Smith of Church Cliff Farm allowed the seal to be kept on land he owned on the Foreshore and the seal continued to entertain visitors for some time. Bonzo died in 1940 of natural causes.

Flither Girls

B ait is vital for fishing, and the fishermen dug large quantities of worms from the beach for this purpose. The location of worms is recognised by the curl of the sand they leave behind on the surface. These together with 'war fish' or 'Razorfish' as they are more commonly known are also dug up; and are identified by a little cup-like depression in the sand with a hole in the centre, which at spring tides are taken at low water and are found sticking up an inch or two out of their holes. In addition, bait named 'lamperns' would be imported from York, London and

Nottingham. This was excellent bait and one-piece sufficed 4 hooks, with each boat taking 200 a week. In 1867, these cost 9 shillings per hundred and the weekly consumption was 6000, from early in February to Good Friday.

The most interesting and lamentable method of procuring bait was by the rough and hazardous labour of the wives, widows and essentially the daughters of the fishermen. Who were relentless in their endeavours and would go out in all weathers to find bait by skeining the mussels (whereby a live mussel is taken from its shell and scooped out). This was very hard and tedious work and from December to June, these strong hardy women and girls would ransack the rocks for flithers (limpets). Unfortunately, due to constant demand, the supply of flithers on the Brigg was very low, therefore, the women had to travel to nearby Gristhorpe.

To shorten the distance, and to reach some parts of these rocks otherwise deemed unapproachable, these resilient bait gatherers descended the cliffs a few yards beyond Newbiggin-Wyke Wyke at a place called 'Chimney Hole'. They did this by means of a rope fastened around their waists and secured by a small and unsafe looking stake placed at the top of the cliff – usually in a hole in the cliff. The women would then descend about 40 feet, hanging for dear life onto the rope, with their feet firmly planted against the perpendicular cliff side, whilst they hurriedly searched for bait.

106

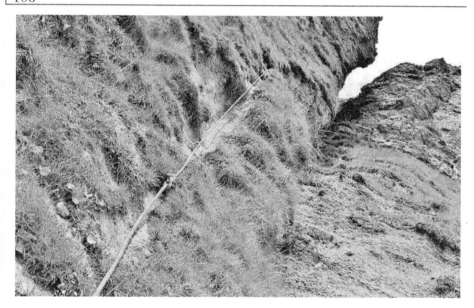

Chimney Hole

In 1863, a steamship named The Volunteer was wrecked on 'the horseshoe rock' close to the cliffs where the ladies sought their bait. Men descended onto the wreckage via ropes and brought back on their backs loads of broken timber and supplies rummaged from the wreck. The flither girls, once they had filled their three baskets, which they called 'mawns', would come up the same dangerous way.

Photograph credit Ian Nisbet

These dedicated women were truly incredible and meticulous. When the Gristhorpe rocks were devoured of all bait, and to satisfy the needs of the fishermen, the women would, week after week, leave Filey by train (they walked before the convenience of the railway) to Scarborough. They would then walk 9-10 miles to Claughton and Hayburn Wyke. They would leave home on Monday-Tuesday and return on Friday/Saturday. During this time, they would take up lodgings, as well as pay for food, all for the reward of the sale of three baskets of bait.

It was a novel sight to witness the girl's return. A carriage was attached to the evening train specifically for them, together with a separate truck for their baskets of bait. Several friends awaited their return, where the distribution of baskets was given to the prospected purchaser. The exhausted yet excited girls were always pleased to be home safe and well and Filey train station was alive with the high-pitched chatter of the Filey dialect, which was often misunderstood, and considered by visitors as

'Moosel gathers chit-chat.'

Fishing Disasters

The orphaned children of Robin Jenkinson (insert) who lost his life on The Research

The immense loss of lives and property on our seas to shipwrecks has been tragic and costly. In such a small community, it was not unusual for families to lose many members of the same family in one event.

Such a tragedy happened on 25th November 1925 when most families were excitedly preparing for Christmas. A great sorrow bestowed over grief-stricken Filey where, following a storm at sea, the entire crew of a steam drifter *The Research* were lost at sea.

One family alone faced a hazardous future, as the father, his two sons, and two of his son's in-law perished, leaving behind them 5 widows and 8 fatherless children. John Robert Jenkinson or Jack Sled (1862-1925) as he was known locally, was the head of the family and skipper of *The Research*. A fearless man who had saved many lives without recognition. His two sons Robin and George were fishermen and sailed with him that fateful day. Robin had six children and George had two. His two sons-in-law were William Cammish and George Crimlisk.

Jack Sled's family were dogged by tragedy. His half-brother, known as 'Dick Sled', Richard Cammish Jenkinson (1846-1918) lost his son and two of his grandsons who were blown up on the *Emulator* in 1919 by a German Mine. Another of Jack Sled's sons James Henry Newby Jenkinson (18921911) was lost in 1911 off Ravenscar aged just 19. He had been working with two other men on the herring coble *Swanland Hall* when it capsized. Jack Sled was a strong swimmer and tried to save the three men by getting them all onto the upturned boat, but as he got one on another would not let go of the keel and fell back into the sea. Sadly, Dick Sled's son James drowned together with another man named George Scales. Sadly, James was about to become a father and the shock of his drowning sent his wife Mary Ellen Jenkinson into labour. His daughter was born shortly after.

It would seem, that the drifter *The Research*, which was owned by Messrs. Melrose of North Shields was an old vessel in poor condition. With hindsight, it is easy to assume that the drifter was not entirely seaworthy. It is known that *The Research* shot her lines and had been fishing off Flamborough Head when the storm struck. Newspaper reports state that the last Filey men to see the crew of *The Research* alive were 'Denk' Major and Mark and Rueben Scotter. Who was on a steam drifter heading for the shore in the face of deteriorating weather conditions. As they passed within 60 yards of *The Research*, Rueben called, 'it's time you were gettin' in, Jack. Run for Brid'. The crew waved to 'Denk' and he waved back. Within an hour, the drifter and the crew were lost. It seems certain that the drifter hit its bottom on 'Smethwick Sands', a large shoal in Bridlington Bay. The sea would have easily swamped her if she were stuck fast. Ironically, if she had stayed offshore in the deeper water she might have been safe.

Remains of the wreckage were washed up two days later, off Hornsea. The wreckage consisted of a fisherman's oil-skin, a gaff (a kind of boat hook) and a piece of wood that bore that marks Y and the figures 42 indicating the registration mark of *The Research* which was Y.H.421. Two fish boxes were also washed ashore with the inscription S.U.S.T Co Ltd, which was the name of the company from Scarborough who was managing the vessel.

The family was a close one, who all lived a few doors from each other in Clifford's Yard and 41 Mitford Street. To add to their suffering, they had not only lost their loved ones but also their breadwinners and sole providers. Being share-fishermen, the bereaved widows were not entitled to a widow's pension under the then Widow and Pension Act of 1925 and had to rely on donations from well-wishers to survive. A fund was quickly started in the press; public sympathy was high, and funds soon accumulated. Scarborough Football Club, Bridlington Yacht club, and The Leeds Mercury were some of the first to offer generous subscriptions. A memorial to *The Research* and all the lives lost is in St Oswald's parish church.

Sadly, in February 1939 Jack Sled's widow Fanny Elizabeth Jenkinson, then aged 76, was told of yet more tragic news. Her grandson had fallen overboard off a motor keel in Whitby and drowned. The sea had already robbed her of her husband, three sons, and two sons-in-law. She had recently been seriously ill, and relatives and friends feared that this latest shock could kill her.

Her grandson, Tom Scotter aged 33, lived with his wife and child in Scarborough. He had been a fisherman for twenty years.

Mrs Jenkinson only had one son left, and after *The Research* disaster, she pleaded with him to leave the sea; he did and took a job as a roadman with the council. She is reported to have said, 'I know what it means, for a man must work, and women must weep. My life seems to have been haunted by tragedy, but if I had my time again. I would still marry a fisherman.' Her epitaph at the family grave at St Oswald's churchyard reads: 'She suffered much but murmured not.'

Filey Lifeboat

In 1823, local historian Mr Thomas Hinderwell started an appeal for Filey to have its own lifeboat and Lifeboat station. Mr Hinderwell was persistent and bombarded many newspapers in York and Hull over his and many people's concerns over the recent storms and the continual loss of life at sea. Following his appeal, contributions began to come in, and in 1823 Filey had its first lifeboat. Unfortunately, this first lifeboat was unnamed but was housed on the foreshore near Cargate Hill. This lifeboat was manned by volunteers and run as a local undertaking unit. The lifeboat relied on sail and oar for their motive power; unlike today where the lifeboat station has the use of an inshore vessel for use on emergencies close to the shoreline.

In 1853, the RNLI took over the running of the lifeboat. Many, lives have been saved by the various lifeboats throughout the years, thanks to the bravery and dedication of the coxswain and the lifeboat crew. In 1863 Filey received its first lifeboat to carry a name; it was Hollon, named in honour of a great benefactor R.W. Hollon – a former Lord Mayor of York. This lifeboat was replaced twenty-one years later by Hollon II and followed twenty-three years later by Hollon III. These three vessels were credited with saving the lives of 169 people, during their 74 years in service.

Old Lifeboat Station credit Emma Guy

Hollon II

The naming of Hollon III 1907

In 1940, Filey received its first motorised lifeboat, *The Cuttle*, named after another benefactor, Mrs Rosemary Cuttle of Rotherham. *The Cuttle* saved 28 lives during its 13 years' service. *The Cuttle* was replaced in 1953 by *The Isa and Penryn Milstead*, which was at Filey until 1968 when it was then replaced by the *Robert and Dorothy Hardcastle*.

The Cuttle 1953 (*Photo: John Holroyd*)

The Isa and Penryn Milstead

The Robert & Dorothy Hardcastle

To be the Coxswain of a lifeboat is a great honour, and Filey is lucky to have had such competent Coxswains over the years. Today (2017) Barry Robson serves the town very well, following in the footsteps of Graham Taylor, who together with the highly trained and brave young people, work as volunteers to protect the lives of people in distress at sea. Throughout the years, Coxswains have included Crompton Wyvill, Richard Cammish, Thomas Cappleman and many more.

There have been many tales of lifeboat rescues over the years. In 1839 the crew of the *Medusa* from Whitby were rescued after a heavy storm. Captain Ruddock was at the helm followed by many volunteers who quickly doffed their jackets, watches etc., and bravely succeeded in rescuing six of the seven men. The seventh, a young eighteen-year-old gentleman insisted in securing some of his clothing and doing so missed his opportunity to jump into the lifeboat, and despite many brave attempts to save him, the young man lost his life.

Filey is indebted to the Coxswain, the crew, and all the volunteers who continue to support this valuable and much-needed service. Together with the many people who contribute to the RNLI, which relies on contributions from the public for its survival.

1

George Dingle Scales Lifeboat Coxswain 1894-1907

Filey Railway

Credit Stephen Eblet

Filey Railway station was opened on 5th October 1846. The first train was operated by the York and Midland Railway Company, which left York station at 11.30 in the morning, heading for its first journey to the coast. This train had five carriages, which were filled with dignitaries including the chairman of the railway company Mr George Hudson, and The Lord and Lady Mayor of York.

The train was decorated with flags and banners and reached Seamer station an hour later then onto its destination: the new Filey station and an eagerly awaiting crowd. Architect George Townsend Andrews, who worked on many railway designs for the eminent Mr Hudson, had designed the station. The station was a single storey red brick structure with a slate roof and sandstone dressings, with a 7-bay main entrance projected from the station. The train shed roof was a common design for Andrew's using a wrought iron truss structure supporting a wood and slate roof.

Arriving at Filey, the townsfolk were out in force. A public holiday had been declared and 400 children lined the street with placards and flags. Mr Bentley had provided barrels of old real ale from his brewery, together with two sides of beef for the locals. Inside the station, the walls were adorned with silk banners saying: 'Success to Hudson and The York & Midland Railway'. Another said: 'Prosperity to the town and trade of Filey'. Afterwards, a procession was held through the town, and Mr Bentley Esq of Ravine Hall laid on elegant carriages to transport the dignitaries to his mansion for an afternoon celebration luncheon.

George Hudson was a financier and a politician who, at the age of twenty-seven, inherited a large sum of money (£30,000) from a distant relative. A relative he barely knew. He invested most of his money into the railways. Thus, he controlled a significant part of this new form of transport, and he earned the title 'The Railway King.' Hudson's financial dealings were somewhat dubious, and he often paid shareholders out of capital rather than profits. In 1849, the railway officials launched an enquiry into his financial dealings, and thus a series of irregularities were found. Hudson suffered severe financial pressure and lost his Conservative seat in Sunderland. Facing bankruptcy, he was forced to live abroad to avoid being arrested for debt, only returning to England when the law for imprisonment for debt was abolished. Hudson never named any of his co-conspirators, who despite reaping the rewards in good times, simply turned their back on him when the going got tough.

Initially, Filey Railway Station included a goods yard, a coal depot and gas works. The fishing industry benefited greatly by the implantation of the railway for the transportation of fish to areas not previously thought possible. Furthermore, the railway opened Filey up as a holiday destination, with people able to travel there and back by train at their own convenience.

Goods traffic ceased to Filey in 1964, and the station was made a Grade II Listed Building in 1988. Recently, improvements have been made to the interior and exterior of the building, and the station is used each day by passengers to travel all over the country.

Education

Prior to the 1870 Education Act, schooling in rural areas was predominantly a matter of chance, cost and the availability of someone willing to offer educational instruction, which would usually be a self-educated spinster from the local neighbourhood.

During the early 19th century education in Filey was deficient, especially for the poor and the working classes. The Wesleyan Methodists who had their own schoolroom on West Avenue (now Dixons) provided day schooling. The Wesleyan school was immediately adjoining the chapel, consisting of two large schoolrooms, one on the ground floor, and one above; each accommodated one hundred infants.

Filey's Mechanics Institute was at 6 Clarence Place, which had a circulating library open to all visitors. In the winter, classes were held for adult members of society who wanted to learn to read and write. Many fishermen took advantage of this, as they'd never had the opportunity to learn before. Educated public members devoted their time and services for free and including for a brief time the notorious Dr Edward William Pritchard (former local doctor, and later a convicted murderer).

Filey did have a generous share of privately run schools. One of the most popular was Clarence House. A private purposely built girls' school run by the formidable Miss McCullum. The school offered a 'High-Class Education' specialising in French and German. The school closed in 1930 after 70 years, when it briefly became a hotel, then a youth hostel. There was a talk at one time that the building was to be demolished, but luckily that was not the case and it is now converted to privately owned flats.

On 28th September 1928, in connection with The Wesleyan Association, London, Hunmanby Hall, the old residence of Humphrey Osbaldeston Esq, opened its doors as a private secondary school for girls'. The first headmistress was Miss Frances Hargreaves B.A, who had a degree in History. She was a minister's daughter, who had previously been assistant head at Kent College for girls.' Miss Hargreaves assured parents of a non-Wesleyan denomination that arrangements would be made for the girls to attend the local parish church. Many alterations had been done to the building, including new bedrooms and sanitary arrangements, new tennis courts, and other playing areas. The old laundry was converted to provide five new classrooms, and the dining hall extended to accommodate 200 pupils. Hunmanby Hall continued as a successful school until 1991. It is now privately-owned flats.

The Crescent, again, offered private schools. There was Brookville School for girls' run by Miss Holmes, and at no 6 Rutland Terrace, and next door at number 4 was Miss Gardiner's Boarding Academy.

The largest private boy's school was Southcliffe Primrose Valley, which was established in 1901, primarily as a preparatory school for boys aged 7-14. The headmaster was Rev. A.H. Gaskell and under his headship, tuition was given for entry to public school. This tuition included music, languages, riding, golf and swimming (the school had its own indoor swimming baths – a luxury for any school). After the school closed the premises became a hotel, then a pub (Churchills) and later part of the Haven holiday chain. Unfortunately, it is now closed and in a dilapidated state of repair.

There was a smaller boy's school was at no 2 Clarence Terrace. Offering only a limited number of spaces for boarders. In 1891, the school advertised 'This school is especially adapted for delicate or backward boys' who require healthy bracing air with home comforts and individual training.'

For Filey children, many of whom came from working-class or poorer families, education was provided by Filey's church school, built-in 1839 on Scarborough Road. The school did not have a good reputation and was considered inadequate for the needs of the pupils. To fulfil the ever-growing pupil population the school was enlarged in 1846, and the premises and facilities were considerably improved. However, the school had serious problems.

In 1879, this school was controlled by Rev. Basil K Woodd the then Vicar of Filey, and the school was open to all religious denominations. In December, the same year, a case was brought against the owners of the school before Magistrate Colonel Prickett at Bridlington Police Court. The claimant was Mr Frederick Buxton the local Sanitary Inspector for Filey. The owners, namely, Rev. Woodd, Mr William Beswick (Gristhorpe) James Haworth, Robert Smith, Robert Cammish, and George Watson all from Filey were ordered to appear. The charges were 'That in or upon The Scarborough Road, in the parish of Filey in the district under public health Act 1875 of the Filey Local Board, and of which premises you are the owners, the following nuisance exists: Namely:

Defective drainage

Want of a winter closet

A supply of water

Ventilation

Damp walls

And a certain contagious disease, and that the said nuisance is caused by you the owners!

The chief defendant was Rev. Woodd who had previously been given the chance to rectify the complaints without escalating matters further, but he chose to ignore this warning, and he did not facilitate any repairs. Therefore, the sanitary board were given no further option than to seek justice in the court.

The circumstances of the case were that in October 1879, an epidemic of Scarlatina broke out in Filey, and the medical officer for health and the inspector of nuisances concluded that the epidemic did not arise in the other church-run schools and could only be attributed to the defective sanitary arrangements of this state church school. Notice had been served on Rev. Woodd to remedy the defective state of the drains etc., but unfortunately, nothing was done.

The claimant went on to describe in detail the state of the school's closets which he stated were built under the walls of the school and directly abutting on the latter. He said the contents had to be seen to be believed and were overflowing into the playground and percolating the walls of the school.

Another complaint was that there was no water connected to the urinals, in fact, he said, 'There was no water laid on to the school at all.' The ventilation was filled with dirty rags, and the walls of the school were damp and unhealthy.

The court case was dismissed on a technicality (the Inspector failed to get the backing of the whole board before issuing proceedings). However, following this report, the school was demolished, and a new national school built in its place on the same land.

Filey Infants/Junior School Scarborough Road Circa 1990

A new Junior school was opened in Mitford Street in February 1900. The land was generously donated by Captain Mitford and the cost to build it was £2,500, which was raised entirely by donations. The school was designed by local man Mr Robson and constructed using only local tradesmen and labour. The school accommodated 250 pupils with a large school hall that also served as a Parish Room. The school closed in the early 1960s and is now Sledmere Court.

Infant's School Mitford Street

In 1946, as the town grew, the two alternative streams were combined with infants, who then started their school days at the Mitford Street school, later going on to the Junior School at Scarborough Road, then finally on to the Secondary School at West Road. During, this period the town was once again expanding rapidly, and new buildings were found on Muston Road, which then became the secondary school (now Ebor Academy). The Mitford Street school closed in the early 1960s, and infants were moved to the Scarborough Road School and juniors to West Road. In 1988, a new infants school was opened on Padbury Avenue and Scarborough Road school was left abandoned, it was demolished in 1999. Private houses were built on the land, and the street named Church View was chosen as a memory to the school.

Filey's Prominent Buildings

Filey has many splendid buildings, and I would not do their history justice by trying to mention them all, so I have chosen a sample. Cliff House, Ackworth House, and North Cliff Villa.

Cliff House

Cliff House – now the Bronte Vinery Cafe and Charlottes, was one of the first houses built in the development of 'New Filey' circa 1824-1855. For a short time, the house enjoyed unrivalled sea views across the 'German Ocean' until the completion of the Crescent in the late 1850s. The original owner of Cliff House was Francis Smith and his wife Eleanor. The Smiths had the honour of sheltering the creator of *Jane Eyre,* Miss Charlotte Bronte, who was a regular visitor to Filey.

Charlotte Bronte loved the sea, which came a close second only to her love of the moors. Charlotte had been ill for some time and thought a trip to Filey and a change of air would do her good. She stayed at Cliff House in June 1852 and wrote to her father from there on 2nd June, in which she beautifully and characteristically expresses a direct reference to Filey. This is a short extract from that letter.

'On the whole, I get on very well here, but I have not bathed yet as I am told it is much too cold and too early in the season. The sea is very grand. Yesterday it was a somewhat unusually high tide, and I stood on the cliffs watching the tumbling in of great tawny turbid waves, that made the whole shore white with foam and filled the air with sand hollower and deeper than thunder.

'When the tide is out the sands are wide, long and smooth, and very pleasant to walk on. When the tides are in, not a vestige of sand remains.'

She also wrote to her lifelong friend Ellen Nussey, on 6th June 1852 again from Cliff House:

'I am in our old lodgings at Mrs Smith's, not however in the same rooms, but in less expensive apartments. They seemed glad to see me, remembered you and me very well, and seemingly, with a great goodwill. The daughter who used to wait on us is just married. Filey seems to me to be much altered; more lodging houses, some of them very handsome, have been built, the sea has all its old grandeur.'

After Charlotte Bronte's death in 1855, Ellen Nussey devoted her life to maintaining the memory of her friend, who she had first met at Roe Head High School, near Dewsbury in 1831. Over the years, they wrote hundreds of letters to each other, which fortunately have eventually made their way to The Bronte Parsonage Museum in Haworth.

Interestingly, the novel *Jane Eyre* was rejected five times from various publishers, but in 1847 Charlotte sent the manuscript to Smith, Elder & Co (London) following advice from her friends William Wordsworth and poet laureate Robert Southey, that 'Novel writing was not the pastime of a lady.' She sent the manuscript under the pen name of Mr Currer Bell. The publishers took the risk and *Jane Eyre* became the masterpiece of fiction we know today.

Miss Bronte is not the only famous writer to have stayed at Cliff House. The writer J. E. Buckrose was a regular visitor to the house in the early 1920s. The novelist whose real name was Mrs Annie Edith Foster Jameson stayed there with her husband Mr R. Falconer Jameson. Cliff House was then owned by Mr Frank Wordsworth Jameson and his wife Ethel Maud Marion Jameson the brother of the writer's husband who had moved to Filey from Hull. J. E. Buckrose wrote over forty books including '*Love in a little Town,* and *The Gossip Shop.'* She used Yorkshire for the setting in all her novels.

In June 1921, a tragedy happened to the Jameson family. At about 2 o'clock in the afternoon, Mrs Ethel Jameson decided to go for a walk to collect wildflowers from the cliff at the top of the Brigg. Robin Jenkinson (who would later lose his life on *The Research*) and Cyril Gannon were at the bottom of the cliffs collecting wood when they heard a thud. Initially, they assumed that a part of the cliff face had eroded and slipped. On closer inspection, they found the lifeless body of a woman sitting upright wedged between two large boulders. It seemed that the body had evidently rebounded after a 200 feet head-on fall. The lady was that of Mrs Edith Jameson who had slipped over the edge. The inquest recorded a verdict of accidental death, and the coroner praised the police officer PC Beckett for his bravery and for making a perilous descent of the cliff by ropes to recover Mrs Jameson's body.

Filey Baths and Spa Company (Ackworth House)

Spa Saloon 1872

During the 18th and 19th centuries, the fashion for spa towns was expanding across the country, and Filey was no exception. With the new buildings on The Crescent Filey was receiving a much larger number of visitors than in previous years and was rapidly gaining a reputation as one of the most fashionable watering-places on the Yorkshire coast.

Filey's hierarchy was concerned that due to a lack of spa facilities in the town, visitors were choosing to travel to the neighbouring towns of

Scarborough or Bridlington, which each had their own spa facilities. In 1861, it was decided to comply with the wishes of visitors and offer these additional facilities. Subsequently, a company was formed under the 'Joint Stock Companies Ltd Liability Acts' named *The Filey Public Baths and Saloon*. The company's Directors were John Wilkes Unett Esq, Chairman, together with The Rev. T. N. Jackson, George Brown Esq, Mr Elisha Elders, Mr William Mosey, Mr Pattison, and Mr Robert Cammish. Two-thirds of the company's shares had been sold, but the remainder were offered for public sale in The Leeds Mercury in 1861.

Building land was secured on The Undercliff (so-called as it was under the cliff) on Filey's seafront, and the property was reported to be built equipped with hot and cold water, showers, and vapour baths. Together with a saloon, reading room, and a suitable dwelling for a manager, the premises were expected to be open in July 1861. In addition, bathing machines belonging to the premises would be available for hire. The cost of the building and all equipment was £8,000. However, this company's success was short-lived as the chairman Mr Unett announced on the 19th June 1874 that the company was to be voluntarily wound up.

An early picture of The Spa

Photograph courtesy of Joanne Cammish

In 1867, the York Herald advertised the property (not the business) for sale by public auction, as 'Valuable freehold property'. The advert stated that 'all the valuable and spacious building comprising: a large saloon, reading and reception rooms, 6 bathrooms, 6 lodging rooms, kitchen cellars and offices'. The advert stressed that the property occupied an unrivalled situation at the centre of Filey Bay, and if desired and subject to the wishes of the overriding spa company, the property could be converted into one or more excellent marine residences. Immediate possession was offered, and the property was hastily secured by Mr Robert Cammish, (one of the Directors of the Filey Public Baths and Saloon Company). Mr Cammish ran the business himself for a further ten years before advertising for a new tenant, however, he did still own the freehold, and various tenants came and went over the years.

In 1880, a Mr Job Charles Chapman, and his new wife Ellen (Ibbetson) were the new tenants. Ellen was originally from Ackworth and wanted to open the premises as a lodging house, Ellen renamed the premises in honour of her hometown as 'Ackworth Guest House'.

However, not everything was plain sailing for the newly-weds. In 1890 their landlord Robert Cammish instructed builders to undertake extensive decorations and rebuilding works to the building, including changing the windows from the original gothic-shaped arches to the more 'modern' square rectangular windows which we still see today. However, there was a dispute with the builder Mr Ruddock, who sued Mr Cammish in Scarborough County Court for £23. 6s. 10d. The plaintiff argued that he was employed to complete extensive decorations and alterations to the property, and whilst most of the contract had been paid there was still this additional amount outstanding. The verdict was for the plaintiff together with associated costs.

Over the years, many applications had been submitted to the Bridlington Petty Sessions for a liqueur license for the premises, arguing that the overspill of visitors from the highly popular Royal Crescent Hotel necessitated an additional license for the Ackworth, but surprisingly the application was continuously refused.

In 1896, a newly formed company named, The Hudson Hotel Company aggressively sought to buy a portfolio of hotels on the Yorkshire Coast.

Mr James Varley, who ran The Royal Crescent Hotel for over two decades, was one of the first to sell his premises for a considerable sum. This was acquired together with Ackworth Guest House, The Ravenscar, Robin Hood's Bay, The Crown, The Royal and The Queens Hotel in Scarborough.

During the Second World War, many properties were commandeered by the armed forces and subsequently, Ackworth Guest House became occupied by The Free French Army. This deployed regiment had a strong presence in the town, and its soldiers liked nothing better than to drink and dance with the locals on a Saturday night.

In 1947, Hudson Hotels leased Ackworth Guest House to CHA Countrywide Holiday's Association and Ackworth House Hotel became the Association's first family centre, but despite this, the centre was for adults only with separate male and female dormitories. No intoxicating liquor was allowed. Prayers were held every morning with a service on Sundays and grace before meals. The evening get-togethers were organised by the host and hostess, who were an essential part of the CHA philosophy, with guests invited to sing, recite or discuss some topic of popular interest. The CHA's communal ideal was further emphasised through the insistence that domestic helpers at the centres were treated as equals and encouraged to join in leisure activities.

Hudson Hotels wound up their company in 1956, and the Royal Crescent Hotel and Ackworth House were both sold to the private sector. The Royal Crescent Hotel became privately owned flats, and in 1982 Ackworth House became a well-respected and privately-owned nursing home as it remained until 2015 when the business was no longer viable, and the property was sold to the private sector.

ACKWORTH HOTEL
(UNLICENSED)
FILEY

A FIRST-CLASS BIJOU HOTEL
beautifully situated on the edge of the Sands.
Bathed in Sunshine. Spacious covered
Veranda facing Sea, from which visitors
may enjoy the air notwithstanding any
inclement weather.

Hot and cold running water in all bedrooms.

BATHING. Direct from the Hotel.
RIDING. Miles and miles of firm Sands.
FISHING. Within 5 minutes of the Brigg.
GOLF. Sporting 18-hole Course within
10 minutes.
TENNIS. Excellent Grass and Hard Courts
within 5 minutes.

Ackworth Hotel

Photograph courtesy Joanne Cammish

North Cliff Villa

North Cliff Villa circa 1895

In 1830 there were only two houses in what is now known as 'New Filey'. The first was Mr & Mrs Smith's red brick residence known as Cliff House (now Bronte Vinery and Charlotte's Cafe) which for many years was the farthest house in a southerly direction. The second was William Voase's villa 'North Cliff Villa', which he had built facing the sea. William was the son of John and Francis Voase, who was listed in the directory of Hull 1823 as wine and spirit merchants and ship owners. The Voase's later became the owners of Anlaby Hall. William

Voase died in 1845, and Sir Thomas Digby Legard of Ganton Hall bought the villa and enlarged it to twice its original size, making it his occasional residence. Following Sir Thomas's death, the property passed to Sir Charles Legard the 11th Baronet. Sir Charles sold the Villa in 1861 to Richard H Foord, the Rector of Foxholes and a Justice of the Peace.

In 1875, John and Margaret Gibson bought the property. John Gibson had previously spent fifteen years as the licensee of The Pack Horse Inn (Queen Street, Filey) and he applied to the Brewster session in York for a liqueur licence for North Cliff Villa. To support his request, he produced a photograph of the premises together with numerously signed testimonials. The Licensed Victuallers Association in Filey opposed the application. Subsequently, the judge refused the licence citing that in Filey there was already a third more licensed houses in proportion to the population compared to that of Scarborough or Bridlington.

John Gibson died shortly afterwards, but his wife and children continued to run North Cliff as a lodging house until the late 1880s.

Filey 1860: Old North Cliff can just be seen at the far top of this picture

In 1890, a spinster named Miss Elinor Clarke bought North Cliff and ordered the immediate demolition of the villa and commissioned the well-known architect, Walter. H. Brierley to design a new substantial building. The villa, completed in 1892, is generally as it stands today.

Miss Clarke died on 4th January 1905, aged 63. In her will, she left the sum of £157,939 (equivalent today (2017) of £17,338,528.42), a considerable amount of money which has for many years led to speculation as to the origins of Miss Clarke's fortune. Previous records recorded that Miss Clarke was a descendant of the wealthy Clark's cotton family from Scotland. She wasn't. She was no relation to this family whatsoever (different spelling of the surname). In fact, Elinor's origins were closer to home.

Elinor Clarke was born in Chorlton on Medlock, Manchester on the 18th September 1842. Her parents were Robert Dennison Clarke and Jane Clarke (nee Skelton). Robert had his own paper-staining business in central Manchester with his partner John Mush. Elinor's mother Jane was a farmer's daughter from Wrelton, Yorkshire.

Paper stainers were found in most large towns and by the mid-nineteenth century, Britain was the world leader in the industrial production of wallpaper, both in terms of design and technology. Manchester arguably was the heart of this industry, and Mush & Clarke were trade leaders. Their premises were at 73 George Street, Central Manchester, they were a well-respected firm, and much in demand. Prior to the mid-1700s only the very wealthy had wallpaper, from China, France or perhaps London. The paper stainer block-printed the paper by hand on relatively short lengths of paper. There was a register pin set in each corner of the wooden block (which they carved themselves) to help locate the second and subsequent strikes accurately, and in this way, a repeat pattern was achieved. The paper might then be overprinted in a second or third colour in just the same way. They typically hung the paper for customers as well. A good provincial paper stainer would offer London and even French papers as well as his own. Until 1836 each sheet was taxed, and paper stainers also had to purchase a licence. Paper-stainers were eventually driven out of business as demand grew for rotary-printed paper in long rolls, printed from engraved metal plates, as we know it today.

This is a token advertising coin the company produced at the time. (1844) To this day tokens bearing the name Mush & Clarke are sometimes found around Manchester and surrounding areas and are occasionally offered for sale on online auctioning sites.

Robert and Jane married on 8th July 1837 at Collegiate Church Manchester (now Manchester Cathedral). The couple had four children, but unfortunately, a daughter Mary died in infancy. The surviving children were Robert Dennison (jr), Eliza and Elinor. Initially, the family lived at 18, Robert Street, Chorlton on Medlock, in a house they rented from a local landowner named Mr Tysick.

Robert and Jane were married seven years when Robert contracted consumption. The disease was rampant in Victorian England, mainly due to poor water supplies, and bad living conditions, and no preventative vaccines available to stop the spread of disease. Consumption or tuberculosis – so-called as it 'consumed' the whole body, with the patient's weight dropping drastically as the disease progressed.

Reports claimed that fresh air was the only cure for this dreadful disease. Therefore, Robert was sent to Scarborough to convalesce with Jane's uncle (Skelton boat-builders, Sandside, Scarborough).

Regrettably, it was too late, Robert was beyond recovery. He died aged thirty-seven in Scarborough on 27th March 1844.

Robert did not leave a will, but he did leave a significant amount of money in the sum of ten thousand pounds. His estate was dealt with by the Prerogative Court of York. The Prerogative Court of York had jurisdiction over Cheshire, Cumberland, Durham, Lancashire and others. This court had the authority to grant probate or administration where the diocesan courts could not entertain the case owing to the deceased having died possessed of goods above a set value in each of two or more dioceses. Unfortunately, not long after Jane caught the same disease and she died soon after.

Following, their mother's death, Elinor, her brother and sister were baptised at St Saviour's Church, Manchester on 6ᵗʰ August 1847. Prior to her death, Jane had made arrangements that her children should be brought up and educated in the care of two spinster sisters Elizabeth and Anne Alderson. The sisters were clergyman's daughters; their father was Rev. William Alderson, the Rector of Everingham. The sisters' brother William was a prison chaplain at Wakefield Prison. William was married to the poet and hymnist Eliza Sibbald Alderson nee Dykes, who wrote many hymns including Lord of Glory, who has brought us, together with and now, beloved Lord, Thy soul resigning. Eliza was also the sister of John Bacchus Dykes, the famous composer who wrote over three hundred hymns, including Holy, Holy, Holy Lord God Almighty.

Initially, the children went to live with the sisters at Strawberry Cottage Matlock, where they are recorded on the 1851 census as 'orphans, and scholars at home'. Ten years later the sisters together with Eliza Clarke (Elinor's sister) are living at Wakefield Prison, Elinor was teaching at a private school in Lytham St Anne's.

Jane's brother John Skelton was also influential over the upbringing of his nieces and nephews and kept a 'fatherly' eye over them. John married Miss Ellen Brown in 1844. Ellen's father Thomas Brown was a wealthy landowner from Greenheys Chorlton-cum-Medlock. John and Ellen had a house built in Timperley, they named Pickering Lodge. This house, an opulent and substantial residence, with immaculate gardens spanned 50 acres of land on Moss Lane and included cottages then named Grove cottages. Unfortunately, not long after the couple moved in, tragedy struck the family once again as Ellen contracted cholera and died shortly after.

Pickering Lodge circa. 1915

The Alderson sisters moved to Filey in 1862, when Elizabeth and Anne purchased 1 Rutland Terrace. The property had previously been owned by architect Mr Elsworth. In 1871, the census chronicles the sisters living there 'on the interest of monies' the other occupants of the house were their niece Caroline, nephew William, and the sisters' younger brother Richard, who was a surgeon. Robert and Eliza were both busy with their own lives in London and Croydon, whilst Elinor was still teaching in Lytham.

The Alderson sisters were excellent teachers, and with their direction, the children received a good standard of education. Robert Denison

Clarke Jr went on to study law at Gonville & Caius College Cambridge, where he graduated with a BA in Law in 1861, followed three years later with an MA. He was called to the bar (Middle Temple) in 1865. Eliza became engaged to one of her brother's friends William Fox-Hawes who was also a barrister. The couple married at St Oswald's Church, Filey on the 1st November 1866. They then moved to Croydon and later had five children. Unfortunately, Eliza died on 3rd April 1881 aged only 43. Her husband William remarried in 1884 and had another daughter Caroline Fox-Hawes.

John Skelton(Jr), had inherited warehouses in New High Street, Central Manchester from his uncle George Wood together with property known as The Polygon (Ardwick). In 1844, John Skelton agreed to let the High Street properties to John Rylands, Manchester's first multi-millionaire. The businessmen agreed that Mr Rylands could join the properties together and let them on a long lease. The property is now occupied by Debenhams. He also inherited property in Chorlton (Chorlton Row) from his father-in-law Thomas Brown which he rented out. Furthermore, John's father died in 1860 leaving him the farm in Wrelton. The cottages attached to the farm were again rented out and the farmhouse itself became a pub named *The Bean Sheaf.*

John continued to invest in property. In Scarborough, he bought and developed *The Pavilion Square,* on which in 1870 the *Pavilion Hotel* was built, (later owned by the Laughton family). In 1860, he had also sold part of his land in Timperley to the Timperley and Altrincham Railway Company, to build a link line between Stockport and Warrington, his name is still preserved at the junction *Skelton Junction* (Timperley). John continued to reside at Pickering Lodge, until 1873, when he met and married Miss Elizabeth Lavinia Theobald, who was the daughter of the Rev. Thomas Theobald, the Rector of Nunnery and Private Chaplain to Lord Palmerston. The wedding took place at Christchurch, Clifton, Bristol, but then the couple moved to London, where they bought two properties, 36 Eaton Square, and a rambling house in Forest Hill Park, Clewer (Windsor).

John made a will, leaving most of his possessions and property to his wife. However, Elizabeth died three years before him. Therefore, the will was amended with the bulk of his estate going to his next of kin, his nephew Robert Dennison Clarke. Elinor, his niece, was bequeathed £5,000. His deceased niece's family(Fox Hawes) were left the rents from the Polygon properties in Manchester which were to be divided between them. John was also a very charitable person and bequeathed a sum of one thousand pounds, the income from which to be distributed at Christmas for the benefit of the poor at Wrelton and Cropton. John Skelton died on 1st June 1886.

Now a wealthy man and a considerable property owner, Robert Dennison Clarke (Jr) sold Pavilion Square, Scarborough and 36 Eaton Square, London, and moved into the house at Forest Hill Park in Clewer. Robert had a housekeeper called Emily King, who had a son called John Skelton Clarke King. What relation the child was to either Robert or John Skelton is unclear. However, in his will, Robert provided for both these people for the rest of their lives (unfortunately, John Skelton Clarke King (a trainee solicitor) was killed in action in 1916 aged twenty-eight) Robert bequeathed the property he had inherited from his uncle and his own estate to his only remaining relative, his sister Elinor. Three years later Robert died. He was fifty years old. The estate now reverted to Robert's next of kin his sister Elinor Clarke.

Elinor, now a woman of substance, sold many of her inherited properties, including Forest Hill Park, Clewer (which backed onto Windsor Castle). In his will, John Skelton's bequeathed a freehold plot of land containing 2 acres 1 rood 26 perches, and the 2 cottages in Timperley (Formerly Pickering Lodge Estate) which at the time of Robert Dennison Clarke's Jr's death was let to Mr Keymer at an annual rent of £45. Mr Keymer was a Manchester merchant and farmer. In October 1893 Elinor Clarke sold the land and cottages to Sidney Keymer, who continued to let them out until his death in 1919. Around this time, Elinor also sold the cottages in Wrelton.

Elinor, together with John Shaw a well-to-do colliery owner of Darrington Hall, Darrington, was involved with the restoration of Welburn Hall in Kirkbymoorside, which had once belonged to the Squire Shepperd of Douthwaite Dale. The property had been left empty for over one hundred years and required extensive renovation. A total of £25,000 was spent on the restoration, which at the time was most probably more than the house was worth. Elinor sold the property to Mr Shaw who went on to complete the renovations, adding a new kitchen wing, servant's hall, stables and a gatehouse.

Exactly, what Elinor's interest in this renovation is at the time of writing (2017) is unclear. However, it may have been political, as Elinor was a staunch conservative, as was Mr Shaw. It could be that Elinor was a member of the Primrose League, an organisation created by Lord Randolph Churchill (father of Sir Winston) whose membership welcomed women, subsequently, many women joined in their droves. These members provided the party with a vast army of volunteers from constituencies throughout the country. Elinor was most likely one of them.

John Shaw provoked notoriety in 1893 when he was defeated in the Pontefract election and brought a court case against his liberal opponent alleging bribery of the electorate. (He was unsuccessful)

LOWER ROSE GARDEN FROM TERRACE. Northcliffe. Filey

The Rose Garden North Cliff

North Cliff remains a very impressive building, with rambling gardens that extend to the seafront. Originally, there was a large greenhouse located where Belvedere Villa once was. (This house was demolished to accommodate this structure and to extend the gardens) Local rumours (not substantiated) say that Elinor wanted to marry Canon Arthur Cooper the 'walking parson' of Filey and that she built North Cliff and its greenhouse to impress him. Even if this rumour were true, Elinor's 'devotion' to the Canon was unsuccessful as the Reverend married the much younger Maude Nicholson in 1891.

The house has a separate cottage, which was occupied by her driver George Gofton and his family. At the back of the house was a piece of land that the locals named Clarke's Asphalt, where Elinor allowed the local fishermen to dry and mend their nets. There was also a separate 'meeting room' which Elinor donated as a community meeting room, primarily used by the boy scouts.

Fishermen mending nets at Clarke's Asphalt circa 1900

Elizabeth Alderson died at North Cliff, Filey age 95 (her sister Anne had died five years earlier). She had been a mentor, friend, substitute mother and educator to Elinor and her family for most of her life.

Elinor Clarke died on 4th January 1905; she was 63 years old. She had suffered from gout for many years. Her obituary says, 'Elinor was a generous friend to the poor, and to the Church of England, and true to the Conservative cause in Filey.' Prior to her death, she had provided new choir stalls for Filey parish church. Miss Clarke was also one of the largest private donors of shirts and clothing to the troops during the war. The Yeomanry guard named a Maxim gun in her honour. At Elinor's funeral, reports say that Canon Cooper was physically shaking and visibly upset when he conducted the service.

The bulk of Elinor's estate was left to her niece and namesake Elinor Fox Hawes, together with the rest of her sister's children. However, she did leave a legacy to her driver George Gofton and to her companion Annie Swann, together with a small amount to her cook and to her butler.

George Gofton chauffeur to Elinor Clarke
Credit Joanne Cammish

North Cliff, the coach house and stables were advertised for sale in March 1905 and auctioned at the Foords Hotel. There was only one bid of £5,000 made by a Mr William Barber of Scarborough. Subsequently, the sale was withdrawn.

The National Union of printers, bookbinders, and paper workers bought North Cliff in 1925, and it became a Convalescent home for its members.

THE HOME FACING NORTH AND KITCHEN GARDEN, Northcliffe. Filey

North Cliff as a Convalescent Home. (Then known as Northcliffe)

In later years, North Cliff was divided into three separate privately owned apartments. However, at the date of writing, the flats have been bought by another private intelligent lady and are again undergoing redevelopment and are in the process of being re-converted to one large elegant house.

Interestingly, Pickering Lodge the house John Skelton had built-in 1850, which was later owned by George Hardy of Hardy's Crown Brewery (Cheadle Hulme) became the annexe to the Auxiliary Military Hospital at

Heyesleigh, the home of Dr Lois Savatard. Heyesleigh Hospital was run by The Red Cross. In 1914, this hospital had 15 beds. The number of beds was increased to 36 with the annexe at Pickering Lodge, which was lent by the then owner Sam Hardy. (Son) To accommodate casualties from the 1st World War, a marquee was erected at the hospital and later an additional hut at Pickering Lodge, bringing the number of beds to 98. Funding for the hospital was helped by volunteers and donations. One scheme was an egg collection organised by the local Church Lads Brigade, whereby the lads collected 6,600 eggs from local farmers and householders. Another scheme was arranged by local school children who collected horse chestnuts, which were to be used as a substitute for grain in an industrial process. All the chestnuts were collected in baskets and then address to 'The Director of Propellant Supplies, Ministry of Munitions!'

Sadly, Pickering Lodge was sold for housing in 1920, and the house bought by the council. Unfortunately, it was discovered that the house was infested with dry rot and had to be demolished. The cottages were demolished on 11 September 1941 after which the land became the public space now known as Moss Park Gardens.

So, what happened next? Elinor Clarke left the bulk of her estate to her niece and namesake Elinor Fox-Hawes, her sister Eliza's daughter. Elinor Fox-Hawes lived in Bournemouth until her death in 1956. Whereby, the monies were then bequeathed to Terence Fox-Hawes a schoolmaster from Bournemouth. Terence died in 1991 leaving an estate valued at £49,564 3sd 11d. (101,666.72) Calculated in 2017. Elinor's other niece Caroline Fox-Hawes also a benefactor in Elinor's will married a Belgium man named Raoul Robichon, who sadly died young at the age of 43. Following her husband's death, Caroline lived at 30A Hanover Square, Middlesex, but died in June 1926 in Paris.

Elinor's housekeeper and companion, Annie Amelia Swann inherited £200 a year for life from Elinor's will. Annie moved from Filey to St John's

Wood, London where she is recorded as living off 'private means.' Elinor's faithful chauffeur George Gofton continued to live in Filey with his wife and family.

In his will, John Skelton's stipulated that the Fox-Hawes children should benefit from the 'chief rent's' from the Polygon properties. However, in 1899 the children were subjected to a matter of theft, the accused was the solicitor who was looking after their interests. An offer was accepted to sell the 'rents' to a Mr Wilkinson who agreed to pay the sum of £4300 for the 'rents' and a deposit of £400 was to be paid on the agreement and the balance on completion. Mr Wilkinson duly paid the deposit as agreed, but the solicitor Mr Robert Wooldenden used this money for his own purposes. It appears that the solicitor had serious financial troubles and had filed for bankruptcy a week before this deposit was paid. Subsequently, the solicitor was arrested and jailed. The sale of the Polygon properties was eventually completed.

Elinor Clarke credit Ian Elsom

Elinor is buried in St Oswald's churchyard close to the ravine. In 1907 a stained-glass window was donated to the church by her nieces Caroline Robichon (nee Fox-Hawes) and Elinor Fox-Hawes in honour of their aunt. A fitting memorial to a memorable and often mysterious woman.

Elinor Clarke Window, St. Oswald's Church

Filey: Public Houses

Throughout the years, locals and visitors have enjoyed a tipple in many of the town's licensed premises. In the mid, to late 19th century, Queen Street was the hub of the community and the place to be. Local fishermen, tradespeople and their families used the various pubs as meeting places to chat and to sample the local ales. At the start of the season, they were joined by an influx of visitors wanting to get away from the grime and industrialisation of the city. The visitors came as they do today, to take in the sea air, relax and mingle with the locals. Also, like today's visitors, they were a much-welcomed sight for a publican after a long hard winter.

The oldest pub in Filey was The Ship. More affectionately known as T'Oard Ship, it was situated at the bottom of King Street (now Queen Street). T'Oard ship was a popular watering hole and licensed premises for two hundred years before its license was confiscated. Subsequently, the pub closed on 1st October 1910. To this day, the T'Oard ship is forever romantically linked to the days of smuggling, which at that time was rife in Filey and Scarborough.

At the time of the pubs closing, newspaper reports state 'The walls of the pub were three or four feet thick; hollow in places and obviously used to store contraband. The beams in the great kitchen were simply a box with a sliding panel. There was a secret chamber under the hearth in the adjoining cottage used as a storeroom to the pub. The upstairs bedroom contained a double floor with peepholes commanding a complete range of Filey Bay.'

Throughout the years, shipwrecked sailors were taken to The Ship for food and warmth, and many a shiny gold coin had passed over the counter as salvage money to local fishermen.

Later in 1910, The Reverend Oxley of Petersham Vicarage, near Surrey, owned the adjoining cottage with its smuggler's hole – once a famous haunt referred to by Charles Dickens, and the author of the poem *T' Fisherfolk of Filey Bay*. (This poem so interested Queen Victoria that she asked for a copy to take with her to Balmoral.) Reverend Oxley purchased the T'Oard Ship together with other adjoining cottages, with the aim of renovating them and turning the buildings into a reading room, a smoking and writing room and a museum. He also intended to use the old pub as a fishermen's shelter and outlook.

The character of the pub was retained, with its famous blue Dutch tiles; an artist from days gone by painted a fish over the mantel. To this, other people added the words:

'O ye whales and all that move in the water, bless ye, Lord,

praise him and magnify him forever.'

The signboard remained above the door; underneath the model of a rigged ship and in a broad Yorkshire dialect said: 'They that go down to the sea in ships, and exercise their business in great waters, these men see the works of the Lord for his wonders in the deep'. Then below the door: 'Oh that men would, therefore, praise the Lord for his goodness, and declare the wonders that he doeth for children of men.'

T' Oard Ship as it is today (2017)

Next door to T'Oard Ship is The Foords. Originally named The New Inn, it was Filey's first purpose-built lodging house. One of the inn's first landlords was Mr Mosey, followed in 1814 by William Mason. The inn boasted it sold a large stock of genuine wines and spirituous liqueurs. The premises were also the pickup point for The Hull & Scarborough Express Company, which ran a daily coach express service to Scarborough. At the time, this service was the only means of transport to the neighbouring towns and villages. This coach left the New Inn at six in the morning arriving at The Talbot Inn in Scarborough at two-thirty in the afternoon.

FOORD'S HOTEL, FILEY.

THE above old-established COMMERCIAL and FAMILY HOTEL is now replete with every convenience.

WELL-AIRED BEDS.

FINE OLD WINES, of the Finest Vintages.

BASS' PALE ALE, in Bottles and Small Casks.

MEUX'S STOUT, in Bottles and on Draught.

FAMILIES SUPPLIED AT WHOLESALE PRICES.

AN OMNIBUS ATTENDS EACH TRAIN.

CARRIAGES OF EVERY DESCRIPTION.

NEW INN, (late MOSEY's,)
FILEY.

WILLIAM MASON,
(Late Servant to Mrs. Bethell, of Rise,)

BEGS leave to acquaint the PUBLIC in general, that he has taken and entered upon the above well-known HOUSE :—which he has entirely new Furnished, and fitted up with every requisite for the comfort and convenience of those who please to visit this pleasant SEA-BATHING RETREAT.— He has also provided a Stock of the VERY BEST WINES, SPIRITS, &c.; to which, as well as to every other department of the House, it is his determination to pay the most particular attention : He therefore respectfully solicits the public support.

N. B. Commodious Bathing Machines, and careful Attendants, during the Season.

FILEY, April, 1814.

THOMAS FOORD,
NEW INN, FILEY,

BEGS to return his most sincere Thanks to the Nobility, Gentry, and the Public in general, for the liberal favours conferred upon him during his residence at the above Inn, and respectfully informs them, that he has added to his Concern, most *Post Chaises* and *good Horses,* which, with care and attention, he hopes to merit a share of Business.

T. F. has also laid in a choice Stock of Old Wines and Spirits ; and has fitted up his Beds in a superior Style, which enables him to render comfortable Accommodation to Families, Commercial Travellers, and others.

The Express Coach to and from Hull and Scarbro', every day, Sundays excepted.

Among the most popular licensees at The New Inn were Mr & Mrs Thomas Foord. The pub was affectionately known by locals by the host's surname: 'The Foords Hotel' or simply 'Foord's'. This name stuck. Thereafter, the New Inn changed its name permanently to remember the town's popular licensees. Mr Foord died unexpectedly in 1839 of a seizure after stabling some horses in the coach house. Reports state that the surgeon Dr Munroe was called but was unable to revive Mr Foord. His widow later married a Mr Robinson from Ayton in 1845.

Foords Hotel (2016)

The Britannia

At 65-71 Queen Street was The Britannia pub. The pub's last licensee was Mr William Gutherless, who had run the pub for two years but had found the business very difficult. This, he stated, was mainly due to the premises being in a bad state of repair, and there was no stabling, rendering it unpopular with travellers. To add to his worries, Mr Gurtherless was charged by the police with keeping the premises open beyond its permitted licensing hours (a regular occurrence in Filey) and for serving the coastguard and his friends after time. Charges that were later dropped as it transpired the coastguard was a friend of the Landlord! Mr Gurtherless could not sustain the business, and the pub's license was discontinued at the 1889 Brewster sessions.

Barrels waiting for collection outside The Britannia photograph courtesy Stephen Eblet

71 Queen Street – you can still see the outline of The Britannia pub

The Pack Horse Inn

OLD ESTABLISHED

PACK HORSE INN,

QUEEN STREET, FILEY.

WINES AND SPIRITS; ALE AND PORTER, BOTTLED AND DRAUGHT.

REFRESHMENTS ON THE SHORTEST NOTICE.

Horses and Carriages for hire. Good Coach-house and Stabling.

JOHN GIBSON, Proprietor.

The Pack Horse Inn was at 78 Queen Street, and its last landlady Mrs Elizabeth Kilby was a likeable and capable host. Elizabeth took the licence for The Pack Horse from John Gibson in 1875. Elizabeth's first husband Henry John Kilby died aged 48 in 1874 leaving her a widow with three children to support. Henry had run The Foords but was declared bankrupt in 1869.

The Pack Horse Queen Street was built in a similar style to the old fisherman's cottages. It was demolished and, in its place, came The Crown Hotel, a bigger and more modern hotel, with additional boarding rooms, and adequate stabling to accommodate Filey's ever-increasing stream of visitors. Mrs Kilby was the Crown's first licensee.

Perhaps, ill-advised Elizabeth Kilby married William M Stubbs a farmer from Cayton in 1881. Business for the Stubbs did not go well, as it is recorded in the Yorkshire Post/Leeds Intelligencer that just four years later in 1885, Mr William Stubbs of Cayton a farmer, cattle dealer and innkeeper of The Crown Hotel Filey had substantial debts and was declared bankrupt. Stubbs had also been charged with being drunk on his own premises and for permitting drunkenness.

Following Stubbs bankruptcy, a few things came to light. Elizabeth Kilby (Stubbs) had previously received a loan from her brother Thomas Wilson who had loaned her £600 plus interest to purchase The Pack Horse Inn. She subsequently married Stubbs, and the Pack Horse was demolished, and The Crown Inn erected in its place. Elizabeth had since mortgaged the Crown Inn to Messrs Woodall & Hebden bankers

Scarborough, but Mr Wilson had not been repaid. After her marriage, her husband William came into the possession of the Crown and all its furniture, but within the provisions of The Women's Property Amendment Act-a husband was not liable for his wife's debts prior to marriage. As Stubbs had been declared bankrupt with many creditors seeking repayment of debts, Mr Wilson was only awarded the sum of £150 plus court costs., which he had little chance of ever receiving.

It seems that Mr Stubbs was not an honest person, as he was again taken to court by his two brothers and sister. Stubbs father who owned the farm at Cayton had died in 1872, William Stubbs was the executor and the terms of the will stipulated that the farm must continue in business for the benefit of the family. This happened until 1880, when Stubbs got a valuation on the farm of £1,360 a share of which, his siblings were entitled. Unfortunately, for them, again William Stubbs was taken to court, as they had not received a penny, the Judge remarking that Stubbs had grossly mismanaged not only his affairs but those of his wife's Elizabeth. William Stubbs died in 1889 aged just thirty-eight.

Elizabeth died in 1895, aged 65. She left two daughters Emily Annie and Grace Elizabeth Kilby and a son also named Henry John Kilby who emigrated to New Zealand following his marriage to Christina Martin in the late 1800s. Elizabeth is buried in St Oswald's churchyard where here inscription reads 'The beloved wife of Henry John Kilby.' No mention of her subsequent marriage.

The Crown Hotel continued as a public house until 2010 when it was closed and demolished to make way for local housing.

The Crown Hotel – closed and ready for demolition

The Grapes, Queen Street

Also, on Queen Street is The Grapes whose landlord in 1877 was Mr William Smith. Mr Smith did not run the pub properly, and at the Brewster sessions in Bridlington was given one week to quit and leave the premises. A week earlier, the police had charged him with permitting drunkenness on the premises. The pub's owner, Sergeant Winpenny, was not impressed and swiftly found a replacement.

Just around the corner from Queen Street, on Church Street, was The Hope & Anchor, which was demolished in 1896 to make way for Laundry Hill. Mr West appearing at Bridlington Brewster sessions on behalf of the landlord applied that the licence is transferred to new premises, which were to be next door to the demolished Hope and Anchor and named The Station Hotel, aptly named to attract visitors who were straight off the trains from West Yorkshire and beyond.

The Imperial Vaults

On the other side of town on Hope Street is The Imperial Vaults, which back in the 1880s was known as The Imperial Bottling Stores. Mr W. G. Long was the proprietor. Mr Long brewed his own beer, bottled it and sold it to the public, and he was also the sole agent for the sale of J. Tetley & Son's celebrated Ales. Mr Long retired in 1881 and the premises were advertised for sale in The Yorkshire Post. The advertisement states that 'the premises at 6 &7 Hope Street consist of two dwelling houses, large wine cellars, a shop, a dram shop and back premises with yards'. Mr Thomas Brunton who ran the business under the name of Brunton & Greaves Imperial Bottling Stores & Innkeeper purchased the premises. However, the business was short-lived, and Mr Brunton is cited in the London Gazette as filing for bankruptcy in March 1892.

W. G. LONG,
WINE AND SPIRIT VAULTS,
AND
ALE AND PORTER STORES,
6, HOPE STREET,
FILEY.

SOLE AGENT FOR
J. TETLEY AND SON'S
CELEBRATED ALES,
LEEDS.
11

In 1893 the premises were bought by a Mr Bennet and renamed The Imperial Vaults (as known as today). Mr Bennet was the licensee but employed a manager, a Mr Proudiouck, to oversee the everyday running of the pub. An incident relating to this management is reported in the Yorkshire Herald of 1893 when Mr Bennet was summoned by Bridlington Magistrates court for allowing drunkenness on his premises. Mr Bennet took great exception to this insisting that it should have been the manager on trial and not his good self as he was not in possession, an objection that was quickly overruled as Mr Bennet was the licence holder and therefore the person responsible. It appears that the police entered the bar late at night and found two men asleep at the bar who appeared to be very drunk and 'senseless'. Witnesses were called who all denied that the men were drunk, their defence was that the men were navvies who were working on the new sea wall and were not able to get lodgings, so they usually slept in the cement sheds. However, about 30 of the men had been allowed to stay at the Imperial

Vaults and were given breakfast and the use of soap and towels whenever they needed them. The manager Mr Proudiouck stated that the two men in question were overtired and not drunk. The bench took some considerable time deciding their verdict and fined Mr Bennet 20 shillings plus costs. Mr Bennet subsequently terminated Mr Proudiouck's employment.

The Three Tuns

Photograph credit Joanne Cammish

One of Filey's biggest pubs is The Three Tuns on Murray Street. The first licensee was Mr Robert Jones who transferred his licence in 1868 to Mr William Barker former landlord of The Britannia Inn, Queen Street. Mr Barker renamed the premises 'Barkers Commercial & Family Inn & Posting house,' advertising that the bar sold the very best quality bottled ales and porter in prime condition. The advert also boasted that there was an omnibus to meet every train. Mr Barker and his family were also the subject of court action and were summoned before Bridlington magistrates for assaulting a Mr Morgan Medd, a man of dubious integrity. Mr Barker & his son accused Mr Medd, a horse-breaker, of robbing people and a fight broke out in the smoking-room of The Three Tuns. The Barkers were found guilty and ordered to pay 20 shillings each plus costs.

Throughout the years, The Three Tuns (and other inns) was often used as an auction house for the sale of land and property throughout Filey. In 1887 A Mr Cammish sold three cottages in Stockdale's Yard which he claimed provided a good investment and rental return, the properties were currently occupied by a Mr Cammish, Mr Baxter and Mr Sayers and their respective families. In September 1944, an auction at The

Three Tuns advertised for sale 320,439 acres of land and buildings known as Church Cliff Farm. The prospectus states that the property has a sea frontage of about two miles and is prime building land. Up until 1899 Filey Golf club was situated here, until a serious landslip forced them to give up their tenancy and move to more suitable premises at the South of the town.

The Star Charity Pigeon Race 1920 (In aid of Scarborough Hospital)

In the late 1800s, The Star Inn on Mitford Street was under the ownership of the Bulmer family. The Bulmer family was a large one and the brothers had quite a reputation for fighting with each other. In 1877, the premises were jointly owned by brothers John & Charles Bulmer who despite running the business together were not getting along. On 12th January 1877, a disturbance was reported to the police and officers were called to the premises where the brothers were fighting. John Bulmer had used a knife on his brother with the intent to cause him harm. Police reported that there was glass all over, and broken chairs and tables. In court, the bench decided that the brothers were 'unfit' to hold a liqueur licence and the couple were fined £50 each and bound over to keep the peace. In addition, the pub's licence was withdrawn, and the magistrates did not allow the pub to reopen until a suitably responsible person could be found. That suitable person was the couple's other brother, James, who was charged sometime later for allowing drunkenness on his premises.

In 1906, the Derby News reports the interesting tale of the strange death of a solicitor from Leeds who had been staying at the Star Hotel. The man, Mr Herbert Armstrong, was found lying on the pavement outside the pub in his nightshirts, with scalp wounds, a broken jaw and elbow, and several cuts and bruises. It later transpired that the solicitor was a chronic alcoholic who had ridden his bike to Foxholes and on his return, had fallen off the bike and sustained these fatal injuries.

There were reports that another pub would be built in Filey, and a Mr Dawson Britten of Hull applied for a licence. Mr Britten told magistrates the pub was to be called 'The Prince of Wales' and would be built near the railway station. Mr Britten assured the bench that he had purchased the land for £375 and that building work would commence shortly. However, it transpired that Mr Britten had only left a deposit of £20 and had insufficient funds to complete the project. The application for a licence was refused.

Seth Gregory & The Belle Vue

The Royal Hotel, Belle Vue Street. (Then North Terrace) Now the site of The Three Tuns car park

In May 1854, The Hull Packet & East Riding Times reported that there had been a serious fire at the Royal Hotel, Filey. The whole east wing of the hotel was on fire, and almost all the valuable furniture in the building belonging to Mr Seth Gregory was destroyed. Mr Gregory, who had only recently taken over as the lessee of the hotel, was slightly injured in the fire and overcome by smoke. However, these injuries were not serious. Scarborough fire brigade attended and ascertained that the fire had started in the fire grate of the dining room, which was only three inches away from the hearthstone – so close that it set fire to the adjoining wood. The damage was done to the hotel and its furniture amounted to £800. Fortunately, Mr Gregory affected an insurance policy on the hotel and its furniture, ten days before the fire. The Royal Hotel was subsequently closed and demolished shortly afterwards.

Seth Gregory was originally from Hull and had moved to Filey with his wife Mary to run The Royal Hotel. Following the fire, he had acquired substantial land on Belle Vue Terrace, and in 1858, The Belle Vue Hotel was constructed. An advertisement in the Hull Packet states, 'These houses are recently constructed and are now ready for the reception of visitors, worthy for nobility, clergy and gentry, there is good stabling, coach houses and a generous supply of water.' The Belle Vue Hotel was competing with the newly constructed hotels and boarding houses on The Crescent, especially Taylor's Hotel (Royal Crescent Court) which attracted Royalty and landed gentry from all over the country.

The Belle Vue (Cliff Hotel)

In 1858, at Bridlington petty sessions Seth Gregory applied for a drinks licence. Initially, his application was not looked upon favourably and opposed. The main reason for the disapproval was that Filey had two thousand residents, and already there were ten licensed premises, which, the bench considered was quite sufficient for a small town. It was also brought into question that The Belle Vue was, in fact, three separate houses, with three separate entrances, and the bench was not sure what Mr Gregory's intentions were. Did he want to cover all three houses, or as one house under one licence? The chairman stipulated that he did not want to give a monopoly to one person. However, if Mr Gregory occupied the premises, and the hotel had one single entrance (for licensing purposes) and if the premises were run as a family hotel, then they believed the licence should be granted. Consequently, The Belle Vue Hotel got its first 'On licence' on 23rd October 1858.

It looks as if either Seth Gregory did not intend to run the hotel himself, or he was finding the business harder than he expected, as on 26th November 1858 an advert appeared in The Hull Packet & East Riding Times, saying. 'To let – recently constructed hotel, 70 rooms, the hotel may be entered immediately, and the rent will commence on 6th April 1859, thereby giving the tenant an opportunity to select his own beers, wines and spirits'. The advertisement also said, 'the present proprietor is retiring from the business"

In December 1861, only four years after opening his hotel, a notice appeared in The London Gazette, requiring Mr Seth Gregory of Filey, in the county of York, the innkeeper, dealer and chapman, to surrender himself to the official receivers and registrars of Leeds Crown Court where he had been adjudged bankrupt. Seth was unable to compete with the affluent hotels on The Crescent and his dreams of running a high-class hotel overlooking the German Ocean finally ended.

On Friday 26th September 1862, by order of the mortgagees and assignees of Seth Gregory, The Belle Vue, land and outbuildings were sold by public auction in separate lots. Seth left Filey with his wife Mary and returned to Hull, where he died shortly afterwards.

Filey's Hotels and Boarding Houses

Taylors' Crescent Hotel, New Filey, Yorkshire

Commanding an extensive View of the Sea

Taylors' Crescent Hotel (now Royal Crescent Court & Bonhommes Bar)

Continuing our journey into Filey's social life, we concentrate on Filey's boarding houses and hotels.

Victorian England brought many changes, with the Industrial Revolution, railways, and the transformation of villages from small farming communities to bustling towns and cities. For the first time in

England, the censuses provided an accurate record of the number of inhabitants of each community together with their occupations. In Filey, the 1801 census recorded the population of Filey to be 505. Following improvements in living conditions, including lighting, sewerage, and drainage the population of Filey increased dramatically.

In the 1830s seven acres of farming land was sold to a Birmingham solicitor John, Wilkes Unett (1770-1856). Unett had a vision for Filey and employed the renowned architect Charles Edge to make his vision a reality. Filey was then transformed into an enviable and fashionable seaside resort attracting visitors from all over the country.

In 1854, Edwin Taylor moved from The Royal Hotel on Belle Vue Street to The Crescent Hotel, which took pride and place at the centre of the newly built elegant Crescent. He immediately renamed it

'Taylor's Crescent Hotel'. His terms were reasonable as advertised in the Hull Packet in 1854.

Terms at Taylor's Crescent Hotel

Board & Lodging in Public Room – 6s

Ditto in Private Room – 7s

Table D' Hote' at Five o'clock. The above all include Attendance, Billiard Table and Bathrooms in the Hotel, Hot Sea-Water Baths, 2s, Shower, 1s. An omnibus and carriage meet all the Trains, Good stabling and Coach Houses.

The hotel was finished to an opulent standard and considered to be one of the finest terraces in England, which attracted the aristocracy and even Royalty, The Guestlist of 1858 boasts visitors such as:

Their Royal Highnesses, the Grand Duke and Duchess of Hesse, and servants.

Her Royal Highness, the Princess Louise of Battenberg, and servants.

The Hon. GW Winn and Mrs of Walton Hall, Wakefield.

And many more.

The Crescent Gardens were not only a place of considerable beauty, but they also provided a source of musical entertainment throughout the season. Advertisements for musicians would appear in fashionable London magazines such as 'The Era,' looking for talented people to play in the bandstand in the Crescent gardens for the summer season. A small charge was levied for entrance to the Gardens, and the original safe used for this purpose is in the basement at Bonhommes (Royal Crescent Court) where due to its weight and size is where it will remain for a long time to come.

The Crescent remains a very fashionable address, and Taylors Crescent Hotel (now Royal Crescent Court) became privately owned flats in 1965 together with the popular award-winning Bonhommes Bar, which to date has survived as the last business still operating on The Crescent.

The Hotel contains about 100 Rooms, comprising large Dining Room and Drawing Room for Ladies and Gentlemen, a Coffee Room for Gentlemen, Sitting Rooms, Bed Rooms, Billiard Room, Smoke Room, and Bath Rooms, &c., &c.

The White Lodge (South Crescent Villa)

South Crescent Villa-now The White Lodge Hotel 1912

At the end of The Crescent stands The White Lodge Hotel. Built-in 1860, South Crescent Villa (as it was originally known) was a private house belonging to Colonel Ackroyd and his wife, from Halifax. The villa suffered a serious chimney fire in 1874, causing severe damage to the roof. Colonel Ackroyd sold the property not long after the fire to actress Madge Kendall (later Dame) and her husband. They renamed the house 'Kendal house'.

The Kendall's at Filey 1912

Mrs Kendall was born in Grimsby the youngest of twenty-two children. The Kendal's travelled the world treading the boards and had five children. It is reported that Madge Kendall was a very cold lady, unable to separate her personal life from her acting career, she became estranged from all her children, and when she died at her home in Hertfordshire in 1935, not one of her five children attended her funeral. Kendal House and all its contents were left solely to Miss Marie Lohr, an actress from Australia; the Kendal children got nothing.

As the years progressed and Filey became a major fashionable tourist resort, private lodging houses and hotels on The Crescent began to emerge. Mrs Barker was well recommended at no 23 The Crescent, offering a dining room and four bedrooms for four guineas a week. Mrs Knaggs on Belle Vue Street and Melville Place were also highly recommended. In 1939, Mr Wilson bought the buildings now known as The Hylands Retirement Home, advertising it as 'Filey's newest hotel' offering access to tennis courts, gardens and all 'mod cons'. Hylands attracted many celebrities who were doing the rounds at Butlin's or Scarborough. Diana Doors stayed there as did The Beatles in 1963 and 1964 after playing at The Futurist in Scarborough.

The Victoria Hotel was also a popular place for the esteemed visitor. In 1937 Mrs Coracan, the owner of this hotel applied to the police for a licence to hold dances for her customers throughout winter, something she had done regularly throughout summer. This application was opposed on behalf of a neighbour, Mrs Gofton who objected to the noise, subsequently, this licence was not granted.

Dancing was all the rage at The Pavilion Theatre (Southdene now Sea Cadets). Andie Caine, the famous Pierrot held many performances there, and the theatre became a popular dancing hall up until its closure in the 1970s. The Grand Theatre (now The Buccaneer) was also a very popular place for visitors, and many performances were enjoyed there until it later became a cinema. In 1911, Filey tradesmen were enjoying a Christmas afternoon exhibition, at the Grand Theatre when there was a mysterious fire which started in the boiler room when several shavings caught fire, had it not been for the prompt action of Filey's fire brigade the building would not be here today, and would most likely have been yet another block of flats.

Pavilion Theatre (Now Filey Sea Cadets)

One of the best memories I have of Filey as a child is at Filey Sun Lounge, which hosted guests doing 'rounds' of the summer season, usually on their way back from Butlin's. The talent contests were particularly good, and I remember practising singing along in my bedroom, using a hairbrush as a microphone. I never won, though, but I do remember a girl from Doncaster winning one year, she had a lovely voice and was called Elizabeth Taylor – unfortunately not the same one. Ken Goodwin was a popular favourite, with his brilliant catch-phrase 'settle down now' a lovely sensitive, funny and professional man and entertainer, sadly missed.

Butlin's Filey closed in 1984, and its closure had a devastating effect on not only the town's tourist industry, but on many of Filey businesses that supplied goods to the camp, such as the local dairy, greengrocers, and Filey laundry. Yet, thanks to the dedication of the landlords/landladies, hotel and boarding house owners who work incredibly hard all year long, Filey remains a popular holiday resort. Credit to them all.

Coroners Inquests & Trials & Petty Sessions

Charles Dickens declared that 'The Coroner frequents more public houses than any man alive.' He wasn't wrong as in the 18th and 19th centuries Inns and public houses were central to the administration of local justice prior to the formation of the police courts and offered an additional source of income to the landlord with increased trade and thirsty spectators wanting to sit in the sessions and fuel their curiosity. The public houses in Filey had their fair share of inquests and petty sessions throughout the years. Here are just a few together with court sessions;

1640

Stephen Martin of Filey appeared at York Castle where he was described as a dangerous rogue, workshy a wanderer and a burglar and was branded on the left shoulder with the letter R.

1863

A Coroner's inquest held before Mr ED Conyers at The Packhorse Inn, upon the body of nine-year-old Sarah Anne Bullamore. The child was sent on an errand, and whilst crossing the road where there was a sharp turn, a horse and cart driven by the son of Mr Prust a butcher from Muston struck the child and she died instantly. A verdict of Accidental death was recorded.

1871

The assistant Coroner Mr WM Wigmore held an inquest at The Pack Horse on the body of a sailor found badly decomposed on Filey Brigg.

The sailor believed to have one of the crews of the ill-fated Unico which had crashed on the Brigg in January 1871. A verdict of 'Found Drowned' was recorded. At the funeral, great respect was shown, and the coffin wrapped with the ship's colours and followed to the grave by Captain Huntley, and Mr Cook overseer of the poor and many local tradesmen of the town.

1898 Filey Shooting

A terrible case was heard at Filey Police Court in 1898. In September that year twenty-one-year-old Edwin Johnson from Muston a chargehand working at Church Cliff Farm, Filey was accused of attempting to murder his work colleagues.

Johnson was attending to his duties together with Mathew Milner, George Coultas and the brother of the farm's owner Mr Smith who was working on a hay-stack in the corner of the farm-yard. Suddenly, without warning Johnson pulled out a gun and fired at the men his target being Mathew Milner, fortunately, Johnson was a poor shot and the bullet narrowly missed his intended victim. He tried another shot and again missed. Johnson in a very excited state the noise of the firing altered other workmen who rushed at Johnson while others ran for the police.

When Johnson saw the Police coming he reloaded the gun and placed the muzzle to his temple and fired. He fell instantly to the ground. The doctor was called for and Johnson was taken to hospital in a critical condition.

The bullet lodged in Johnson's brain was removed, but he lost an eye and the prognosis was that in time he would eventually be completely blind. Johnson was remanded in Jail when he was fit enough and taken to trial for attempted murder. At the trial, the judge took all the circumstances into account and fined Johnson ten-pounds and bound him over to keep the peace for one year.

Flying

Mr Hucks filling up with Petrol before going to Scarboro'. 17.5.11 FISHER. FILEY

The broad cliffs and wide sands of Filey attracted amateur aviators from all over the country. Thus, in May 1910, permission was granted by Filey Urban District Council to Mr J. W. F. Tranmer of Scarborough to use Filey sands for the purposes of aviation training. Mr Tranmer erected a hangar and bungalow at Primrose Valley, together with a twelve-foot-wide slipway, which was constructed to facilitate the winching of aircraft down to the beach 60 yards below. Two 25 h.p Bleriot monoplanes were brought over from France and delivered to Filey by rail, and a flying school was opened nearby.

The first recorded flight from Filey beach was on 25th July 1910 by Bradford man Mr William House who was a member of the Northern Aero syndicate. Mr House had planned his first Filey flight to coincide with his honeymoon. However, this flight was not entirely successful as he smashed the wing of the plane and ended up soaked in petrol and trapped in the wreckage. It took several local people some time to extract him from the plane. Not the best way to start a marriage.

It seems that Mr Tranmer lost interest in his enterprise as he advertised the property for rent in Flight magazine. Subsequently, the business was rented to Mr Robert Blackburn, who renamed the school Blackburn Flying School. Mr Blackburn was originally from Leeds and he is credited as one of the first pioneers of British Aviation. One of Blackburn's flying instructors was Essex-born Mr Bentfield Charles Hucks who learned to fly on Filey beach.

Early in 1911, a prize of fifty pounds had been offered for the first pilot to fly between Filey and Leeds. Hucks made several attempts at this but was not successful. In June 1911, he had a serious accident when flying between Filey and Scarborough, when the propeller of his plane fell off. The plane lurched forward and crashed headfirst onto Filey beach. Mr Hucks sustained injuries to his head and legs, and some spectators received minor injuries, but the plane was a complete right-off.

In December 1911, another instructor of the Blackburn Flying school was Mr Hubert Oxley, who together with his assistant 32-year-old Robert Weiss a rag-merchant from Dewsbury decided to set out to fly to Leeds in his 'Mercury' plane to win the £50 prize. Before, setting off to Leeds Mr Oxley took a preliminary flight around Filey. The weather was clear with a slight frost in the air. Scores of spectators had lined the beach to watch the flight, which was a success until Oxley decided to descend on the beach just in front of the lifeboat shed. The plane was at a height of about 80 feet when suddenly it buckled backwards, and the machine dived onto the sands. Mr Oxley was shot head first out of his seat like a projectile, landing 15 yards away on his head. He didn't stand a chance. His neck was broken, and death was instantaneous. Robert Weiss was pinned under the plane and was unconscious. He had serious injuries including a fractured skull, broken thighs and ankles, and internal injuries. He was immediately taken to the coastguard station, where he died shortly after.

A spokesman for Filey stated that Mr Oxley had intended to take as a passenger his engineer Mr A. C. Hunt who was already seated on the plane when Mr Weiss appeared asking to be allowed on the flight. Mr Oxley had reluctantly agreed. Mr Hunt gave an engineer's statement at the inquest where he stated that Mr Oxley was fond of diving down with his engine working instead of volplaning. Mr Hunt said that on one occasion when he accompanied him, he had warned Mr Oxley that he was looking for trouble, but Mr Oxley had just laughed!

The tragic deaths did not deter aviators, who continued their quest to fly between Leeds and Filey. Mr Brereton, a pilot from Bristol replaced Mr Oxley who with the engineer Mr Hunt attempted to win the Royal Aero Club pilot certificate. Two new planes were purchased including a Blackburn monoplane which was fitted with an improved Isaacson engine; they were housed in the hangar on Primrose Valley.

In 1912, a letter was sent to Filey Urban Council from The Blackburn Flying school stating that owing to the expense of keeping machines at Filey and with the lack of any financial support from the town, the company advised that it would have to relocate to another part of the country. The company asked the council if it would be prepared to see its way to subsidising the cost of the hangar expenses, then it would continue with its experiments with a hydroplane in Filey Bay and would also conduct the trials of its new military machines. The company argued that if Filey remained an aviation centre, it would be of significant material benefit to the town.

The council decided that as a public body, it could be of no assistance in the matter. Mr Blackburn moved his operation to Hendon in September 1912.

1916, saw the Blackburn & Aeroplane Motor Company move to Brough (Near Hull), where it built a new factory. Through the war years, the company flourished, especially with the proximity of the Humber close by, which was ideal for the launching of seaplanes. The company continued to grow and in 1939 became Blackburn Aircraft

Ltd. By 1949, the company amalgamated with General Aircraft Ltd. In 1955, this company won a contract to supply new aircraft to the Royal Navy. The aircraft, the NA39, known as The Buccaneer was very successful and was in production for twenty years. In 1960 the company then became The Hawker Blackburn division of the giant Hawker Siddeley Aviation Combine, which in 1965 became Hawker Siddeley (Brough) and later became part of the British Aerospace Kingston-Brough Division.

The aircraft hangar at Primrose Valley was initially used for storage by the military battalions engaged in coastal defence duties. The hangar was sold in 1921 to Mr Frederick Parker an engineer from Hunmanby, who dismantled it to use as housing for his tractor engines. Unfortunately, the hangar was not fit for this purpose and was re-sold.

Filey can be credited for having a major influence on the aviation industry. Furthermore, Mr Hubert Hucks was acknowledged as being the first pilot in England to loop the loop. This happened on 25th July 1914 when Hucks flew at great height over Hunmanby then completed the loop over Filey Railway Station roof. To commemorate Filey's involvement in flying, a plaque has been erected on the seafront.

Accidents & Murders

The Fall of Three Young Men

B etween the years of 1862 and 1909, three young Filey men fell to their deaths in different circumstances.

On the afternoon of 8th October 1862, fifteen-year-old Thomas Henry Suggitt, the son of Thomas and Zillah Suggitt (nee Agar) was on Filey Brigg, a place he often went to search for objects for his hobby as a nature lover.

This afternoon he was searching for artefacts for his sister's aquarium. Thomas was a well-respected and studious young man who had just secured a place at a London College to study Civil engineering.

Thomas was last seen alive heading towards the cliffs on the north side. He would have had to climb up to the ridge, a frequently used but very dangerous mountain like a pathway. A dangerous part of the cliff is known as the 'neck' aptly named and is just wide enough to give a foothold, albeit a very treacherous one. At the time, the best way to pass the 'neck' was to take a quick sprint. Thomas, it seemed, had succeeded with this deathly dash and ascended to an altitude of approximately fifty feet, and tried to position his collection boxes higher up the cliff when he lost his footing and fell backwards. Thomas rolled from ridge to ridge and tried desperately to regain his hold; unfortunately, he lost his grip and fell over the edge to the rocks below. His body was found shortly afterwards, and reports confirmed that death occurred instantly.

Amos Proctor was born in Muston in April 1848. He was one of eight children born to Thomas Proctor and Sarah (nee Edmund.) The Proctors were a notorious family and Amos was the twin brother of the iniquitous Maria Proctor (Stonehouse) who was bludgeoned to death by her drunken, violent husband Samuel Stonehouse in Filey in 1894.

Amos's mother Sarah was also no stranger to crime, she had appeared in front of the judge at Bridlington petty sessions in 1867 for stealing a pair of men's boots belonging to Mr Thomas Vasey of Filey and was fined twenty pounds.

In 1870 Amos was working at J & E Jacques Flour mill in Scarborough. Amos had gone to the upper storey of the mill to attach the strap to the revolving 'sack tackle' when he got himself jammed between the upright shaft and the revolving apparatus. A colleague quickly tried to raise the alarm and shut the power off. Amos was eventually freed, and taken to his home in Muston, where despite the best efforts of Dr Taylor the local GP Amos died in the early hours of the following morning aged just twenty-two. The inquest recorded a verdict of accidental death when it transpired that Amos had attempted to put the strap on the four-wheel with his foot.

Amos's sister, the ill-fated Maria, could not accept the death of her beloved twin brother, and this is most likely the reason for her rapid decline and why her life spiralled out of control. It might explain why she turned to drink, a major contribution in her eventual murder. (See a Scandalous Woman)

*

John Rawson was the youngest son of William and Elizabeth Ann Rawson nee Maulson, who resided at 32, Queen Street, Filey.

Aged nineteen John worked as a plumber for Councillor Gibson. On 20th May 1909 Mr Gibson, had sent John and a colleague Mr Lindley to a job at 3, Belle Vue, Filey, a property belonging to Dr and Mrs Croke of Hull. John had done various jobs for the Croke's in the past and they were very fond of him, and Mrs Croke had specifically requested Mr Gibson to send John as he had recently fitted some gas fittings for her and general maintenance. On a fateful evening, Mrs Croke requested if John was available to clean her windows.

John was used to heights and climbed onto the V-shaped ledge. Unfortunately, he lost his footing and fell off the ledge onto his arm, then onto his head, cracking his skull on the pavement. John was taken to his sister's house, a Mrs Webb at 2, Rutland Terrace, but despite some hope, he did not regain consciousness.

An inquest was held on the 28th May 1909 where a verdict of accidental death was recorded, and no blame attached to anyone, just a stern warning of the dangers of cleaning windows at such a dangerous height.

A Scandalous Woman

Maria Proctor was born in Muston in 1848; she was the fourth of eight children born to Thomas Proctor and Sarah Edmund. Maria had a twin brother Amos, who died in an industrial accident whilst working for R & B Jacques flour mill in Scarborough in 1870 at the age of twenty-two.

Maria already had an illegitimate son Thomas William Proctor when she met Samuel Stonehouse from Scalby. The couple married in 1878 and they rented a seventy-two-acre farm at Low Moor, Hunmanby from Mrs Dale, Scarborough. Samuel and Maria had three more children, Ellen Elizabeth, Samuel Dixon, and Sarah. Ellen Elizabeth died in February 1889 age ten.

By all accounts, Samuel was a quiet, hard-working man, but when he and Maria started drinking which they often did, their quarrelling and fights were notorious. Both were no strangers to the Bridlington petty sessions, and both appeared before the judge in 1878 on entirely different charges. Samuel (milk-seller) fined £1.00 plus costs for using a horse whilst in an unfit state – the poor horse fell twice whilst attempting to draw a bathing machine out of the sea. Maria (milk-seller) appeared later in the same year for watering milk down by ten per cent and was fined £2, plus 12 shillings' costs. This could account for the reasons they moved to Filey, eventually ending up at a small cottage at the end of Barnett's Yard, off Queen Street.

The neighbours were used to Samuel and Maria's drunken arguments, and Maria's screams of 'murder' were often heard when she took a battering off Samuel. Maria did her fair share of the battling and the couple's landlord, John Barnett, referred to Maria as the worst of the two and called her a 'scandalous woman'. Maria could match Samuel when it came to drinking, and many times Samuel would hand most of his wages to Maria on Saturday afternoon, but by Sunday evening, it was all gone.

On Saturday 27th October 1894, Samuel had been working as a bricklayer's labourer erecting new buildings, next to the Spa Saloon. At lunchtime, he called into the Imperial Vaults on Hope Street with friends. Maria soon came looking for him knowing that Samuel had collected his wages; she wanted her share so that she could also go out drinking. Samuel and Maria continued drinking in the pubs of Filey, and Samuel was so inebriated in The Star that the barman refused to serve him any more alcohol. In the meantime, a reasonably sober Maria went home to do some baking.

When Samuel eventually went home to Barnett's Yard the fighting started. The couple's two children Sarah and Samuel Dixon were present, and the neighbours took no notice of the throwing of pots and pans – a normal occurrence at the Stonehouse's on a Saturday night. Samuel Dixon was becoming increasingly concerned when he witnessed his father striking his mother across the head with a firebrick. The brick split in two and fractured Maria's skull. Samuel Dixon ran to fetch his uncle Edmund. Edmund returned with Sergeant Clarkson, who witnessed Maria lying on the sofa moaning the words, 'Oh my poor body, he has kicked me to death.' Blood was flowing from the wound at the back of her head, and her arm was broken where she had tried to defend herself. Dr Orr, the local doctor, attended but it was too late. Maria, aged 46, died from her wounds shortly afterwards. Samuel was subsequently arrested and taken into custody at Hull jail for the murder of his wife.

In November 1894, Samuel Stonehouse stood trial at York assizes. A post-mortem carried out on Maria revealed that she had a diseased heart and liver, and despite thirty-nine wounds found on Maria's body, the court doctor Dr Stephens, reported that Maria had died of shock. The couple's children who were now in the custody of their uncle Edmond – all said that their mother drank. The judge and jury considered this evidence and convicted Samuel of the lesser charge of manslaughter and sentenced him to fourteen years' penal servitude. Samuel Stonehouse wrote to the Secretary of State to appeal his sentence, all the facts were considered along with many letters praising Samuel's previously good character, hence his sentence was reduced to twelve years.

When released from prison Samuel returned to his hometown of Scarborough and died in 1920 at the age of seventy-two.

Five Children Drowned on Reighton Sands

Credit Ian Nisbet

In October 1902, Mr Luke White, coroner, held an inquest on the bodies of four of the five children who were swept away by the tide at Reighton, Filey, whilst they were playing on the sands. In his opening statement, Mr White said it was one of the most painful inquests he had ever had to conduct. A great disaster had fallen upon not only the parents of these poor unfortunate children, but a veil of sadness had encompassed the whole town. On Friday afternoon (August 1902) these young girls were playing on the beach enjoying themselves, when shortly after they were all lying dead in the same cottage they were staying at. A very painful scene for all involved. Every attempt had been made to save these children.

Credit Ian Nisbet

Mrs Lavinia Taylor, mother of three of the girls had lost her entire family. She had been visiting her husband's sister Mrs Webster who lived in a cottage at Reighton Gap. Mrs Taylor had stayed a fortnight and was due to go home to Leeds the day before, but the children had insisted that they stay longer. The cousins were in the habit of going onto the sands and digging sandcastles on their own.

Credit Ian Nisbet

On Friday 29th August, the girls had made a sandcastle and taken off their boots and stockings and were having a paddle in the water. Three-year-old Hannah Mary Webster was reluctant to go paddling but was persuaded by her cousin nine-year-old Clarissa who said, 'Come on don't be a baby we're having fun!' Five minutes later the five children were surrounded by water; frightened, they started to scream. Hearing the screams, the mothers saw the perilous position of their daughters and at once threw off their boots and attempted to reach and rescue them. One of the mothers went almost up to her neck in the water, but when she found that the water was carrying her away, she was forced to relinquish her attempt. The mother's frantic screams alerted a Miss Harper who knew the sands and quickly took off her dress and jumped into the sea to rescue the girls, but again to no avail. Mr Cass a violinist from Scarborough, tried to save the girls, but before he could get to them he went underneath the water and had no choice but to save himself. Screams were heard from the children as a large wave engulfed them and carried them all off together. The last sight was the girls' heads bobbing up and down then no trace of them at all.

The five children were:

Martha Alice Webster aged 11

Hannah Mary Webster aged 3

Their cousins, daughters of David and Lavinia Taylor of Kirkland Place, Beeston, Leeds.

Lillian Taylor aged 12

Elsie Taylor aged 7

Clarissa Taylor aged 9

The part of the beach where the children drowned was almost deserted at the time, and nobody appears to have noticed the children were in danger in time to save them.

The coroner did not find it necessary to record any further evidence and praised the mothers, Miss Harper and Mr Cass for their conduct and bravery. The coroner and the jury expressed their heartfelt sympathy to the bereaved parents. A verdict of accidental drowning was returned. R.I.P Little Girls-You are not forgotten.

Credit Ian Nisbet

Filey is truly a magical place. The jewel of the Yorkshire Coast, but as we have read about in this book there are also many dangers – from strong tides, dangerous cliffs or simply sunburn on the beach. Remember to watch for incoming tides and be careful always. Above all have fun and don't forget the sunscreen.

*

If you enjoyed reading this book please consider leaving a review and rating on the site where you purchased it. Please tell your friends about *The History of Filey and its People* and help keep the history of the wonderful town alive. This helps tremendously.

Thank you

Sources of Information

Thank you for all the excellent resources for help in compiling this book. Many of the titles are out of print, but several were made available from Google digitised archives. A valuable and addictive source for my research has been The British Newspaper Archives. As some of the photographs are old their quality is sometimes impaired.

A Historical and Descriptive Guide to Filey. W.S. Cortis. 1858.

Buildings of England, Yorkshire, York and East Riding. Nikolaus Pevsner. Penguin Books. 1972.

Domesday Book and the East Riding. F.W. Brooks. 1966.

Fearon, Michael. *Filey*. 1st ed. Beverley, East Yorkshire: Hutton, 1990. Print.

Filey and its Church. A.N. Cooper. F.W. Brooks (The Gentleman's Magazine) Accessed online 24/1/2017.

Observations of Filey as a Watering Place. E.W. Pritchard M.D M.R.C.S. George L Beeforth, 3, St Nicholas Street, Scarborough 1858.

Shipwrecks and The Yorkshire Coast. Arthur Godfrey and Peter J Lasey Dalesman Books. 1974.

The Filey Handbook. Rev.Arthur Pettitt MA. Loxley Bros. 1868.

The History & Antiquities of Filey in the County of York. John Cole Printed and Published by J. Cole 1828.

Websites.

"Borthwick Institute for Archives - Borthwick Institute for Archives, The University of York". York.ac.uk. N.p., 2017. (Elinor Clarke)

British Newspaper Archive". Britishnewspaperarchive.co.uk. N.p., 2017.

Web. 26 Jan. 2017.websites.
https://www.facebook.com/groups/photosoffiley/Accessed 20162017.

"Gristhorpe Man - University of Bradford". Bradford.ac.uk. N.p., 2017. Web. 26 Jan. 2017.

Hull Packet. A Scandalous Woman. Accessed 5/7/2015.

London Evening Standard. 18/2/1857. 'Filey's Iron Church.' Accessed 4/4/2016.

"Matlock And Matlock Bath: Kelly's Directory, 1855". Andrewsgen.com. N.p., 2017. Web. 26 Jan. 2017. (Re Elinor Clarke)

Newcastle Chronicle. 16/3/1866-Filey 'Harbour of Refuge.' Accessed 2/3/2016

The London Gazette. 'Filey Harbour Company.' Accessed 10/5/2016.

Trove. n/a. au/newspaper articles 68721534-Filey Flying.
www.myprimitivemethodists.org.uk (Accessed 21/2/2017)
www.christianitytoday.com (Accessed 21/2/2017)

Email-

Filey Town Council.

The Jorvik Centre-York. Cockayne, Kevin. Filey. E-mail.

Waterson, Edward-Elinor Clarke-Email-Elinor Clarke.

Theobald, James-Email. Elinor Clarke

Printed in Great Britain
by Amazon

78664852R00129